All About Meetings

All About Meetings

A Practical Guide

by

FERN LONG

OCEANA PUBLICATIONS, INC.
Dobbs Ferry, New York
1967

CONTENTS

FOREWORD

It has been my good fortune to have fallen into a career which has brought me frequent contact with a phenomenon which, while it is not uniquely American, has certainly reached its fullest development in our democratic society. Indeed, without it we should never have become such a society. I refer, of course, to The Meeting as it includes and implies every type of gathering, purposeful to greater or lesser degree. I have been participant in, and perpetrator of such meetings, and whether one or the other, I have always been a critical observer of both strengths and weaknesses, the former often raising a meeting to the heights of the sublime, the latter sinking it into the very depths of the ridiculous.

Not only have I borne the responsibility for both fiasco and success, as planner and executor, but upon occasion I have been speaker at various types of gatherings, and in that capacity again have had opportunities to experience and to observe both the good and the bad, and to learn, I hope, from both.

I should say that fiascoes occurred early in my career, and I learned from them, usually the hard way of embarrassment and self-recrimination for not having thought of everything that should have been thought of to prevent such situations. Not that there are no longer failures; they still occur, but not so frequently.

It is only human to wish to pass on to others the lessons one has learned from experience, and that is admittedly the reason why this book is being written. After having been exposed to such manifestations of poor planning as long-delayed openings of meetings, ill-prepared physical settings, last-minute rushes to do what should have been done days and even weeks before, confused seating, bad lighting, bumbling and often tactless introductions, non-functioning microphones, awkward and ungracious dismissals, I conceived the wish to do what I could to help those who might find themselves in the position of program planner, chairman of arrangements, staff member working with a board, or board member working with a staff, in setting up meetings of one kind or another.

Forewarned is sometimes forearmed, and if we know the obstacle course, we stand a better chance of running it without mishap. Even though there is no substitute for experience, conscientious direction-giving and taking can help.

This little book will attempt to be a thoughtful guide to good meetings.

One word about what it is *not*: it is *not* a "handbook for clubmembers," giving the rules of procedure from the alpha of a group's birth to the possible omega of its demise for carefully detailed reasons. Books like this definitely have their value, exist in considerable numbers, and may be found listed in the appended bibliography.

INTRODUCTION

With increasing interest I read this little book on what a program planner should not only know but do. I have had so many contacts with program planners and speakers that I could not visualize anything new on the subject of meetings; however, I underestimated the author, whom I have known and admired for many years.

Dr. Fern Long, valued member of the Cleveland Public Library staff, originated the Live Long and Like It Library Club programs which have contributed so much to the happiness of senior citizens. She has planned many other programs both inside and outside the Library, and is a most adept program organizer. Moreover, as a platform personality she has endured the discomfort and embarrassment of unskilled handling. From a well of experience she has distilled this clear summarization of what to do, when and how to do it.

Taking the mistakes of herself and others under consideration, Dr. Long has included in her analysis, in addition to basic planning needs, anticipated pitfalls into which any planner or chairman may fall, warning against possible dangers that threaten those who do not follow a careful and well-reasoned procedure.

This makes the volume a valuable work for practical application as well as reference, to be read, absorbed and followed to the benefit of program chairmen no matter where they may be or what exigencies they face.

Among the hazards of which she warns, may I add my own experience in addressing a service club meeting of lim-

ited duration. So much inconsequential matter was dis-
cussed that I was left exactly three minutes in which to
present a half-hour address. And this is by no means an
uncommon experience.

Above all, see that this volume has a key place in your
club library. Read it. It is something every clubwoman and
yes—every clubman—should know.

HARLOWE R. HOYT

1

WHY MEETINGS?

There is no creature under the sun more purposefully gregarious than man. The beasts that hunt in packs have a single objective: the prey. The bees that swarm have one aim: production. Only the gregariousness of man is multi-purposed, and without this basic trait most of his great accomplishments would be neither conceived nor achieved. So far as we know, man is the most efficiently communicative of all his fellow creatures. It is this compulsion to communicate which would seem to lie at the root of all organization, from the most elementary children's club to man's crowning attainment, the creation of the state. There has been progress when communication was successful, chaos and tragedy when communication broke down.

Man has an inborn desire to talk about things, to pass his thoughts on to his fellows, to dispute the ideas of others whenever he has enjoyed the freedom to do so. This will to communicate has made man more than the animals, and is carrying him beyond the stars.

From time immemorial people have gathered together —to wage war, to worship, to govern, to learn, to teach, to enjoy. When civilization flowered, assemblies proliferated: the Greeks had their agora and symposium; the Romans had their forum. The Dark Ages were a time of separateness, and when they ended, the process of communication had to begin all over again.

It is probably true that in no place and at no time in the world's history did the meeting attain the functionalism nor reach the degree of development which it has in our own country.

In the first place, it was the most efficient instrument in the forging of the new republic. Here we were not at all different from other nations that have accomplished political changes, either good or bad, for there has been no revolution that has not been preceded by bringing the people together for exhortation, planning, and action.

When students from other countries come here to observe our customs and institutions, they are invariably struck by the number of institutions in existence, as well as by the number and variety of meetings which take place not only in our large metropolitan centers but also in our towns and villages. From the earliest days of settling this part of the world, to the later waves of immigration, to the most recent coming of displaced persons, those who came learned quickly that meetings served a number of good purposes. They offered the social opportunity to come together with others who shared a common background; they were the most efficient method of passing along information to a group of people; they were the only way to arrive at the solution of problems which the whole group shared; they were the best and sometimes the only medium by which an old culture could be kept alive and a new one created. Often a meeting provided the means of accomplishing tangible results necessary to the welfare of a given community. The Town Meetings, the church socials, the educational and cultural meetings, the husking bees of our earlier days have their counterparts today, and these counterparts exist for the same reasons as did their predecessors.

Motives for holding meetings are what they have always been:

I. They are an instrument for passing along and exchanging important information.

Even though developments in the areas of rapid transportation and mass communication have added speed to the dissemination of certain kinds of information, still the radio and television are not interested in the exchange which takes place on the level of a service club or League of Women Voters meeting. Indeed, by their very nature they are not able to effectuate such an exchange, for they offer no possibility of a face-to-face encounter.

II. They may be a problem-solving device.

When meetings are held in certain professional, political, business or industrial areas, their main purpose is to attack and solve a problem. Anyone who has participated in the group approach to seeking a solution must be fascinated by the process, the developments and changes which take place as the question, idea or problem goes under the hammer of many minds.

III. They give the opportunity for social contact and for alleviation of the loneliness which most individuals feel.

Many factors are making the "loner" a rare phenomenon in modern society where increasingly the group is the pivot around which most activity revolves. Anyone who works with groups quickly learns that loneliness is a great motivating factor in attracting membership.

IV. They present the possibility of adding to educational and cultural backgrounds, and the avowed purpose of many meetings is just that.

As complexities in modern living multiply, there is more and more need for the educational meeting. Television has not accepted its potential role in this area, and the agora or forum is still as necessary as it was in ancient Greece and Rome. Even educational TV lacks the flesh-and-blood dimension, and is to a "live" meeting as a movie is to a stage play.

V. They may themselves accomplish, or help to bring about, the achievement of tangible ends.

The husking bee is a thing of the happy past, but fund-raising is very much of the present. Meetings are an indispensable part of every campaign of this sort.

There may be other answers to the question "Why Meetings?" Anyone who plans a meeting should have his own well-defined conception of why he is doing so.

2

WHAT IS A MEETING?

The dictionary defines a meeting as simply a gathering or an assembly. But what a variety of possibilities those few words cover!

Actually, there are probably four main types of meetings: the business, the civic or political, the educational or cultural, and the purely recreational. Let us take them one by one and see what each may include.

I. The Business Meeting.

The thing to remember about this type is that some are solely business, and that others combine the business aspect with something else. We may consider both under this heading.

A. The Committee Meeting.

This category is listed first because it is the one that involves the fewest people, and may be regarded by some as the simplest of the meeting types. As a matter of fact it is not, and the committees which make up an organization are its very foundation stones. If the committees do not function and produce, the organization does not really survive as a healthy body.

A committee may be either appointed by the president of an organization or voted in by its membership. The former procedure is the one most generally practiced. It may be a standing committee —that is, a permanent committee taking care of a matter which is a continuing concern, or it may be an "ad hoc" committee appointed to give its attention to one single question or problem. After

4

an answer or solution is found, the ad hoc committee is dissolved.

By the very nature of a committee, all its meetings are business meetings. Even when it is directed to produce a purely social result, its instrument is still the regular business meeting, conducted systematically and logically.

When a committee is appointed or elected, it should be given a clearly stated charge. Its work becomes much simpler if it knows definitely what it is expected to do. If an organization has a constitution and by-laws, the functions of the standing committees are usually stated there. In that case the president of the organization may simply give to the committee chairman a copy of the section describing his job.

However, when the president has appointed an ad hoc committee, then he really should present it with a charge, for example:

1. The Committee on Opportunities for Older People to Serve is given the charge to investigate (a) how many older people in Blankville want volunteer assignments, and (b) what volunteer opportunities there are for our older people.

2. The Banquet Committee of X Association is given the charge to make all arrangements for the banquet in connection with its annual convention: engage room, order menu and decorations, plan seating, provide music.

3. The Film Festival Committee of the Blankville Women's Club is given the charge to handle all details concerning the showing of award-winning 16mm films in the Civic Auditorium, October, 19—. The Chairman may appoint subcommittees at her discretion.

The committee chairman should read the charge to the members, or better yet, see that each has a copy of it, so that it is clearly understood by everyone.

A committee meeting should be conducted at least as meticulously as any other large meeting.

The chairman should give the members adequate notice of meetings—at the very least a week ahead of the date and time set. In fact, when it is very important that every member be present, a telephone check is frequently made in order to arrive at a time convenient for all members. This is especially necessary if the committee is small and exceptionally high-powered.

The chairman should have a carefully prepared agenda, with a copy for each member, if possible. More will be said about agenda and their importance in a later chapter.

No matter how small a committee is, minutes of its proceedings should be kept and submitted to all members either in written or oral form, preferably the former. Without a careful record of what goes on, it is too easy for misunderstandings to arise. It is always good to have a record to look back upon. Also, it keeps absent members au courant with what has gone on, and saves the time of informing them during a session.

Committee members appreciate short, businesslike meetings. It is possible to be less formal, less restricted by parliamentary rule, in a small committee meeting. Members may decide to reach agreement by consensus, rather than by formal motions and voting.

In fact, there is a definite trend towards informality in all smaller meetings. It is usually the middle-aged clubwoman, trained during the period of strict parliamentarianism, who requests, even in the smallest committee meetings, motions and seconds, and insists on repeating them before they are voted upon. Sometimes this amuses, but oftener irks, her committee members, who are busy men and women.

B. The Club Meeting.

It is said that just before World War II, Japan sent a Commission to the United States to study our most influential opinion-makers. At the conclusion of the study, women's clubs headed the list.

To be sure, of the thousands of clubs which have sprung up in every American metropolis and hamlet, the great majority are women's clubs. But not all. The men's service clubs, advertising clubs, sales clubs, et al., certainly swell the organization count substantially.

The regular club meeting is seldom exclusively a business meeting, and conversely, only rarely does a club hold a meeting which has no business aspects whatsoever.

The minimum business meeting consists of the call to order, reading and approval of minutes, treasurer's report, consideration of old business, introduction of new business.

With this disposed of, many clubs proceed to a program of some kind, educational, cultural, or recreational.

However, it is the business meeting, no matter how brief it may be, which is the bone and sinew of this type of organization. The common purpose, the common interests, articulated directly or indirectly through the business meeting, are what give the club its continuity.

Some organizations which have rather brief and perfunctory business sessions at their regular meetings have taken to setting aside one entire meeting a year and devoting it exclusively to business. This is an especially efficient practice in the case of those clubs which plan their own programs.

C. The Board Meeting.

What is referred to here is not necessarily the board of a business corporation, but rather those boards associated with the health, welfare, educational, and religious agencies which exist in every American community, large and small. Most of these boards are elected, either by the people in regular elections, or by procedures set up within the organizations themselves. In some instances a large parent body appoints the board of an agency which stands in a satellite relationship to it.

These boards are distinguished by the fact that their interests and purview are implied by the character of the body they serve. That is, a board of education is committed to serve the public schools, a library board the library, the board of the Council of Churches to fulfill whatever is required of it relative to the churches of a given community.

Probably even more than our clubs, this particular type of organization is uniquely typical of our democratic society.

As has been said, its concerns are dictated by the nature of the parent body, so its agenda will always contain matters directly related to the welfare of that body. These matters can be very far-ranging, as anyone who has ever served on such a board will attest. Budget, salaries, personnel, research projects, problems of the staff, relations of the organization to the community—all these and many more items become the concern of the citizen whose privilege it is to serve on this kind of board.

Meetings of these bodies are always business meetings of the most concentrated and purposeful kind. Minutes and financial reports are kept for them just as they should be for every organization. However, in these instances they are usually taken by a professional secretary in the employ of the organization. Customarily these are mimeographed and distributed to members well in advance of the next scheduled meeting.

There is an aspect of these boards which differentiates them from any other type of organization. That is, they work closely with certain designated staff members of the parent body: the executive director, the superintendent, however the salaried head of the agency may be designated. At its best this system offers a means of intercommunication between lay representatives of the community and professional members of a complex organization. For the professional the board member is a means of moral support, a means of interpreting to the wider community the objectives as well as the needs of the agency which both serve. Usually, and perhaps inevitably, the board member is almost completely dependent upon the staff member for information and often for guidance.

At its worst the system can make of the board member a kind of Charlie McCarthy of the administration. There are instances where even the motions which the board members are to give have been carefully written out by a staff member.

D. The Staff Meeting.

Again this is always a business meeting, and it is always work oriented. Although this kind of meeting is very different in purpose from all those which have so far been mentioned, an agenda should be prepared for it just as well as for the others, and a careful record of what goes on should be made and preserved.

Staff meetings are usually conducted by the staff chief, although some heads experiment with letting other staff members take turns in carrying out this responsibility.

The form may be one, more than one, or all of the following:

1. The Report Meeting.
    This type has a clear objective. It is designed for the direct presentation of reports by individual staff members.

    This is a very helpful kind of meeting, especially if a staff has engaged in a new and experimental kind of program in which a number of people are working alone in different areas. The exchange of information, with opportunity for questions and discussion, has a unifying effect upon a staff, as well as keeping it informed.

2. The Decision-Making Meeting.
    At first thought, it might seem that this category would involve staff only at the topmost level, but this is not necessarily so. Decisions of varying degrees of importance must be made on every level.

    At its best, this kind of session draws together the thinking of all the people on a staff, and eventually forms that thinking into a decision.

3. The Creative Meeting.
    This is very likely the most difficult of all to conduct. In a permissive atmosphere new ideas are supposed to flow forth freely in what has come to be known as brainstorming.

    There is a wise saying, *ex nihilo nihil,* and those who participate in such sessions must have something to begin with if original and creative ideas are to be generated.

II. The Civic Meeting.

This may take place on the initiative of one, or of only a few people, of an official of a city or an organization.

In other words, there are no rules that dictate when or how a civic meeting is to occur. It may have one of several objectives:

A. To celebrate a significant event or anniversary.

Very likely most cities in the country, and many in the world, have observances of United Nations Day. In a good number of instances this takes the form of a luncheon meeting or an evening meeting. But at whatever time of day it is held, it offers a good example of a civic meeting.

B. To honor a native son or daughter.

From time to time most of our towns have a local hero to whom they want to pay honor. Cleveland in the summer of 1965 had the perfect example of such a local hero when Robert Manry came back after sailing the Tinkerbelle across the Atlantic. More than a thousand people turned out to the civic luncheon for him, and thousands more lined the streets to wave to him as he rode along in an open car, his little boat behind him.

Retirements of distinguished citizens, or the presenting of awards, may offer other reasons for such civic gatherings.

C. To celebrate a community achievement.

When a new public building is opened, those who gather at its dedication may be said to comprise a civic meeting.

When a fund drive reaches its goal and goes beyond it, those involved in the success will sometimes call a civic meeting to celebrate.

The triumphs of an athletic team are often the occasion for calling a meeting to honor its members and to underscore their achievement.

D. To call attention to a community need.

In these days when such concentrated and widespread efforts are being dedicated to the achievement of the Great Society, it is not difficult to think of examples of this sort of meeting on every level from the street club type to one which would involve those in the highest spheres of influence.

These are actual examples of such meetings:

1. Citizens of a slum area which was in process

of undergoing "urban renewal" met several times to consider what might be done to have their garbage collected oftener than once a month. They were well aware that those who dwelt in other quarters of the city had a collection once a week.

2. Parents who lived in an area where a branch library was needed met together for more than a year to devise a plan of action whereby such a service might be secured.

3. A group of influential business men formed an association to accomplish revitalization of an inner city area which had become commercially dead. This was affecting adversely not only the business community, but the entire metropolis.

In all three examples cited it is obvious that someone must have taken the lead, that more than one meeting must have been held, and that if they were successful, action must have followed discussion and formulation of plans.

In the first case, spontaneous neighborhood interest brought about the meeting; in the second, the P.T.A. took the lead; in the third, the president of a large department store made the first steps towards organization.

In all, the problem at hand determined the agenda of the meetings, and certainly all formality was kept to a minimum.

III. The Educational or Cultural Meeting.

In a way, all meetings are educational, but under this heading the kind that is being considered is the one whose sole aim is to educate, to edify, to add knowledge or insights, to enrich the lives of those who attend, to offer inspiration and stimulation.

Frequently an organization's annual meeting will fall into this category. There are also organizations whose entire program is built on the objective of enlightenment for its members. This type of program is a direct descendant of the old lyceums, the old Chatauquas, which offered welcome opportunities for adult education to those who lived far from the cultural centers of our then sparsely settled country.

Here are a few examples of this type of meeting:

A. Book and Author luncheons or dinners, which take place in some of our larger cities. People come to these partly out of curiosity concerning the personalities, but just as much to learn and to be stimulated.

In many cases these affairs are sponsored exclusively by one of the local newspapers. However, in a number of instances the local public libraries and book stores work with the newspaper to promote the success of the enterprises.

B. Travel programs are offered widely, and they are popular. Although they may be classed as pure entertainment, they are more than that, for they bring information about other places and other people. Moreover, those who attend them frequently do so in order to prepare themselves for their own travels.

C. Book review meetings are certainly educational, and if they are done well, stimulate the listeners to read.

D. Foreign policy associations and councils on world affairs devote their meetings entirely to educating on the subjects implicit in their names, and what could be more important at this particular moment of history when our country has attained a pinnacle of awesome power.

E. Social agencies more than ever are now feeling the need to educate the communities they serve about the problems which they have faced for many years, and of which the general population is only now becoming acutely aware as we have entered a time when not only are the problems seething and boiling over, but when the searchlight of federal attention is being played upon them. More and more meetings are being held to inform the citizens at large about subjects which no longer seem remote from any of us, as they once did, when "across the tracks" was far from the thoughts of leading citizens.

F. Organizations like the League of Women Voters have exclusively educational meetings, with the focus always upon some well-defined domestic or international issue.

G. Meetings that concentrate upon the arts—appreciation of music, of dancing, of the graphic arts—these are expanding and diffusing as we become more mature as a nation and as our government increasingly follows the pattern of the older cultures which have traditionally assumed governmental responsibility for the development of the arts.

IV. The Entertainment or Recreational Meeting.

We all know what this popular type of meeting is, and we all enjoy it. The magicians, the jokesters, the song-and-dance men—whether they are strictly amateur or high-priced talent brought in for the occasion—their objective is to entertain, to lighten the mood of the audience and for a little while allow the people present to leave behind them the routine of every day.

Although carefully prepared agenda are needed for the last two types of meetings, recorded minutes of them are not always made.

If an educational meeting is addressed by an outstanding speaker, often a verbatim transcript is printed or mimeographed and made available to those who were present. Increasingly tape recordings are made of outstanding programs, and preserved as long as their usefulness lasts.

No matter into what category a meeting falls, however, there are certain requisite procedures which apply to all of them and which must not only be learned, but also applied, by anyone who bears the responsibility for a meeting of any kind whatsoever.

3

THE PLANNERS AND THE PLANS

Who are the meeting planners? First of all, the president, chairman, executive director, or whatever the head of an organization is called. When he takes office he must know that the ultimate responsibility for the performance, good or bad, of the group which he heads, rests on him. Still, while he has the moral responsibility for this, he cannot possibly perform in all the capacities necessary to assure success.

Therefore, the head of an organization must give very careful thought to the selection of those committees whose efficient functioning will insure the favorable termination of whatever enterprises it embarks upon. The program committee is one of the most important and choice of personnel who are to assume its responsibilities should never be made on a subjective or emotional basis. For example, "Mrs. Doe will not be president this year and we should find something interesting for her to do so that she will not feel slighted and left out. We'll make her Chairman of the Program Committee." Mrs. Doe (or Mr. Doe) should *not* be made chairman of a program committee unless she (or he) has the qualifications that will make a *good* chairman. Certainly this particular committee chairman holds a key position in the executive body and should be selected with special care. All too often this kind of care is not exerted.

The person who is made accountable for programs should:

not be a procrastinator,

have an ability—which would make him kin to a detective —to ferret out program resources and follow leads,

be persistent and willing to work,

never yield to discouragement.

Some organizations have two committees charged with responsibility for programs: one for the regular meetings, and another with the sole responsibility of planning and arranging the large annual meeting. But no matter how this is handled, the head of the organization should check frequently with the program committee chairman to make sure that the assignment is being filled properly. There is nothing worse than the empty feeling a president can have when he comes within a few weeks of an annual meeting date and suddenly realizes that there is no program for it. This happens from time to time.

There is wisdom and logic in the practice of appointing these two program committees instead of only one, for while the planning approach to each is substantially similar, the pressures on the two committees, and the intensity with which they work, differ.

The same basic principles apply to both:

Start your planning and actual work as soon as you are appointed. When one takes office in May or June, six months or twelve months seem as if they are ages in the future, but time has a way of slipping by very quickly, and nothing is more upsetting than the last-minute panic of a procrastinating program planner.

Select your theme, or themes, carefully. Certainly the subject of your programs should bear some relationship to the general objectives of the organization. With some organizations this relationship is clear-cut and plainly named (a novel club will not study poetry, and vice versa). While considering themes it must also be recognized that some programs are themeless, and that the planner must concentrate on producing a variety of interesting programs which bring to those who attend them a many-faceted experience.

Any responsible program committee will want to get

some idea from the membership as a whole of what subjects it would like to delve into during the committee's term of office. The chairman might request time at a regular business meeting to mine these ideas from the general membership. Some organizations (not many) have a built-in procedure for involving their entire membership in program planning and decisions. That is, they set aside one or more full meetings to be devoted completely to this objective. One technique of learning a group's preference is by questionnaire. A wise chairman will create in the group an atmosphere which is permissive enough that members feel entirely free to submit their suggestions and wishes for programs.

Certain basic courtesies must be extended to those who contribute to your program, whether it be a single one or an entire series, and should be kept in mind from the beginning. They will be described in detail later.

Now let us consider some suggested procedures for the regular programs. They may be of two kinds. A goodly number of clubs (usually women's) depend upon their own members; others bring in speakers from the outside, often expecting these performers to contribute their talents gratis.

The committee planning for the former has the easier task. These are suggested steps:

Make a chart of the dates to be filled.

Determine which members are to be assigned subjects, and list them. In many instances a rotating procedure has been established, so that a member may be called upon to perform only every two or three years.

Choose your theme and your subjects. This is really the most difficult step of all. However, there are many themes that lend themselves to breakdown by subject, and here your local librarian can be of great help to you. Public libraries have a long tradition of being of assistance to women's clubs which once upon a time were the only program planners.

Gradually men's groups too are seeking this type of help.

Current magazines and newspapers can be sources of program ideas, and a good planner keeps up to date on that kind of literature. In fact, a clipping file may be of real help to a program chairman.

Here are a few suggestions of subjects which may be broken down into a number of programs:

The history and culture of a country, or countries, in which the members may have an interest.

One group, for example, presented a year's program called *The Splendor and Glory of Spain*. In the course of one year the music, art, literature, history, and architecture of that romantic country were studied. A film about long-ago Spain, *The Cid*, had just appeared and awakened new interest in Spain, enough so that some members traveled to that part of the world. The same attention may be focussed on any country.

The War on Poverty.

There has seldom been a subject which has attracted such widespread interest and controversy as the current heroic attempt to eliminate poverty.

It is multifaceted, including both urban and rural slum clearance, both urban and rural renewal, education at all levels, vocational training, juvenile delinquency.

Books have proliferated on every phase of this subject, and in fact are among the most interesting products of the publishing trade at this moment of writing.

New Developments in Education.

This subject is closely related to the one above.

There is great concern currently about public education, which goes beyond our anxieties as to why Johnny can't read, although that too still concerns us—especially when Johnny can't read or write even after he has finished high school and is 25 years old or older.

Our Country's Relations with Other Countries.

This is a phase of our national life about which there is widespread interest and anxiety, from the war in Vietnam to what is going to become of NATO. The subject will be too serious for most organizations to care to develop, but many will feel challenged by it, and it is second to none in importance.

Biographies.

Nearly all of us are interested in the lives of other people, and this subject lends itself to infinite development. The lives of our presidents' wives, of writers of any given era or country, of statesmen, of composers or artists, the entire field provides an unfailing supply of book material, and even films.* Producers of educational 16 millimeter documentaries have brought out excellent biographical films in recent years, and if you have access to a sound projector, films on many subjects are a great resource.

The Book Review.
Although this is probably the commonest of all programs, it is still one of the best.
It is really no easier to plan than any of the others, for the program committee has the task of selecting the books to be reviewed, keeping in mind the special interests of the club and its members.

In making any program plans there are a few simple cautions:
Don't try to cover too much ground in one meeting, or even in one year.
If you choose a big topic, concentrate on one important phase of it.
Don't make your program too complex. A simple listing of a subject in simple words is most effective.
Be wary of tackling subjects about which you know nothing at all.
Always be sure that adequate material exists on the topics you are assigning. If books are involved, make certain that they are still in print, or, if they are scarce items in your public library, that they may be obtained in paperback.

Now, if you as chairman of a program committee must secure speakers from outside your membership, you have a more difficult task.

Again you will need to determine the theme upon which programs are to be focussed, or if you are to have greater freedom to present a variety of subjects. We have already noted that the character of an organization will dictate to a large extent the subjects to be covered. Also, the time of year at which a meeting occurs will suggest the program. The most obvious example of this is the one at the Christmas season.

---

* See your public library for information on film sources.

You will need to make a chart also of dates to be filled, with some tentative suggestions for each.

If your organization provides you with a budget with which to pay your speakers, you are fortunate. At the same time, it is your duty to apportion the funds wisely. Some organizations, even though they have a budget for paying speakers, try to get a certain number of free ones, in order to pay a few outstanding performers higher fees.

Many organizations, however, depend upon getting programs at no cost. If funds are budgeted for a speaker, they are likely to be earmarked for the annual meeting.

Program chairmen who operate in metropolitan areas are lucky, for talent resources multiply in proportion to the size and diversity of a community. But even in small communities there are some waiting to be discovered.

How are they discovered? Your first port of call in your talent search should be your public library. Some have organized files of names of local people who are willing to speak, listing also their subjects and whether or not they charge a fee. Some performers who ordinarily charge will contribute their services to certain types of religious, charitable, or educational institutions.

Your local newspaper is a good information provider. Sometimes you will find a story about a distinguished visitor to your area who might be persuaded to speak for your group. Clip pertinent articles and make a file for either immediate or future reference.

Chambers of Commerce often keep files of community resources, including speakers, and can be a mine of information.

Make friends with your local booksellers. Authors are often very engaging speakers and always interesting personalities. Sometimes a talk to a local group may be combined with an autographing party in the bookstore.

Make an inventory of your community program resources: museums, public schools, libraries, social agencies, travel bureaus, public utilities, chambers of commerce, manufacturing plants, zoological gardens, colleges, special schools teaching the arts, department stores, newspapers, specialty stores, garden centers, law enforcement and federal agencies which exist now in such numbers. In short, make as complete a survey as your ingenuity will allow. You will find upon investigation that a number of these enterprises offer speakers as part of their public service. Put the information down on paper or on file cards, so that this valuable material will not be lost when you go out of office.

Some communities periodically issue a kind of chart of resources for program planners. In Cleveland, for example, the Public Library, the East Ohio Gas Company, and the Chamber of Commerce join forces to bring out a detailed listing* of program aids available throughout the area, most of them free.

More and more organizations of different types are including the services of speakers as part of their public relations program. One of the best examples of this trend is the Ohio Bell Telephone Company which advertises its Speakers' Bureau along with the weather report.

Don't forget that there are other kinds of programs besides speakers and performers. Films, slides and recordings make a welcome change now and then. Again, free films and records are available from a number of sources, and your public library should be able to direct you to them. Also, the State University in your area may have an audio-visual department, as many of them do, and an inquiry directed to it can bring you helpful information.

A word of caution to those who schedule free speakers or free films: never book them unless you have some idea of their quality; otherwise, it is possible to find yourself in the embarrassing position of presenting a low-grade program.

We noted that frequently an organization has a separate committee to plan and produce its annual meeting. That plan usually includes bringing a paid speaker whose fee is met by an item included in the budget, by selling tickets,

---

* To obtain a copy send a five-cent stamp, your name and address to the Adult Education -Department, Cleveland Public Library, 325 Superior Avenue, Cleveland, Ohio 44114.

or by having a meal function—luncheon or dinner—for which a larger charge is made than the actual cost of the meal. If enough attend, the cost is easily met through that surcharge.

The person in charge of planning the annual meeting should start work immediately upon appointment. His committee should decide exactly:

> Whether it will be a meal function or not.
> Where and when it will be held.
> The type of program it will have. Entertaining or serious? Will there be music?
> How much can the organization or its members afford to spend on the affair?

Nearly all larger organizations desire to bring in a distinguished speaker from outside the community for the annual meeting. When this is the case, early planning is especially important, for experience shows that one gets many rejections before one gets an acceptance, even when one is prepared to pay a speaker generously. The people who make a career out of speaking are usually in great demand, and often set their fees high in order to reduce that demand.

There are a number of excellent lecture bureaus from which one may obtain speakers, and a list of these will be found in the appendix. Your public libraries may have their brochures on file. If not, you may write directly to the bureaus for information on available talent.

From experience and observation many of us know that it is possible to come within a few weeks of a meeting and still not have a speaker, even though every planning rule has been followed. There comes a point when you have to give up trying to get your speaker by letter and resort to long-distance telephone. To forestall getting to that point it is well to use the telephone from the beginning and consider the expense simply as part of the overall budget.

It must be said, too, that there are times when all the preliminaries have been executed in perfect order, only to have a blow struck by fate a mere few days before an event.

This has happened to all of us who have much to do with meetings. On one occasion the speaker was engaged, all details taken care of, and three days before she was to arrive at her hotel, a wire was received saying that she had stomach ulcers and was in the hospital. Not only that, the substitute came down with influenza the day before the meeting. What could be done? An excellent local speaker was secured, and those who attended went away with glowing praise. However, the anxious chairman nearly had a heart attack and was so ill the night of the meeting that he could not attend.

You will need to decide whether your speaker and whatever reports you have to make at your meeting will be an adequate program. Incidentally, keep business reports to as much of a minimum as you legally can at the annual meeting, which in many instances is attended by non-members who are bored by prosy details.

Soft dinner or luncheon music is pleasant if you have a meal function. Often this can be contributed by local talent —students, or people who love to perform and who, of course, are good at it.

Decorations, seating, and other physical arrangements are all very much part of what must be planned if a meeting is to be successful. But these details are so important that a later chapter will be devoted wholly to them.

Some communities, acting in the belief that program planning is a subject of interest to many organizations and agencies, have regularly produced Program Planning Institutes, sometimes annually, sometimes less frequently, depending upon the apparent need.

This has been done cooperatively with many groups working together, or it has been done by a single Federation or Council of Clubs. A local adult education council, an art museum, a public library, board of education, federation of women's clubs, a nearby college, council of churches, a welfare council have pooled ingenuity and resources to produce such institutes in some of our larger cities.

Subjects presented parallel those which have been considered in this chapter. An Institute has a great advantage in that it makes possible face-to-face situations in which those who have either resources to talk about or instruction to give are confronted by those who want to learn and who will have the opportunity for discussion and questioning of experts.

These Institutes have usually been presented in the late Spring or early Summer, after elections and after program chairmen have been appointed. It is an incomparable means of preparing for the coming year. Sample programs of two such Institutes may be found in the appendix.

4

YOU AND YOUR SPEAKER

There is a very special relationship which exists between the program chairman and the speakers he secures either for routine meetings or for the large annual affair. It is a formal and ephemeral relationship, but it is a close and important one as long as it lasts, and it should be pervaded from beginning to end with the utmost courtesy and consideration.

Let us take a hypothetical situation and follow the procedure of engaging, presenting, and thanking the speaker, from the very first contact to the final note of thanks.

You may secure your speaker either through a lecture bureau or by direct contact. If it is the former, the speaker is under contract to the bureau, and it will arrange all details. The bureau will also forward a contract to you and work under strictly business arrangements. You will get a statement of your speaker's fee and also instructions as to the payment of other expenses, such as travel, and meals en route. If possible, it is best to pay for everything in a lump sum. Some organizations have found themselves with large bar bills and long-distance telephone bills when they have assumed responsibility for their speaker's hotel expenses.

The lecture bureau will also instruct you in the matter of paying a fee. Usually they ask that a check, made out to their bureau, be given to the speaker immediately upon completion of his task. The bureau takes its commission out of this fee, and the speaker is given his agreed percentage.

But now supposing you are going to get in touch with a speaker directly, one who is not being managed by any agency. You may want someone you have heard at another meeting and who was so good that you wish to present him to your own organization in order that its members may have the pleasure of hearing something that you have already enjoyed. You may have read a certain author's book and been so interested in what he had to say that you would like to hear his views face to face and perhaps have the opportunity to question him and discuss his ideas. There may be a statesman or politician who, you feel, should be heard by your organization. There may be an outstanding local person whom you would like to present to your membership.

How would you proceed? In the preceding chapter the use of the telephone, local or long distance, was recommended. Only in the case of the author may this not be the most effective approach. To reach him you may wish, as has already been suggested, to make your initial advance through your local book store, or conceivably through the author's publisher. New authors especially are often glad of opportunities to enlarge the circle of those who are acquainted with them and their work. Older, more established authors are difficult to engage as speakers unless the occasion is really something very special, or unless they really love to talk. Many writers do not enjoy speaking and avoid it whenever they can.

If you decide to approach your prospective speaker by telephone, be very sure of what you want to say and how you want to say it. It is a good idea to have this written down in outline form before you dial. Also remember to have paper, pencil, and a calendar handy when you call.

The direct and simple approach is best. Even though you are paying for the call, unnecessary verbiage is not appreciated by busy people. State your name and your connection with your organization. Tell your prospective speaker at once that you are calling him because you wish him to speak. Describe the occasion for which you are inviting him, give him the date, time and place, as well as an indication of the subject upon which you would like him to speak.

Be businesslike about his fee, and ask him very directly what it is. There are occasions, however, when it might be appropriate to tell the prospective speaker just how much is available in your budget for your event. Then he can say immediately whether or not he is willing to appear for that amount, and you will not be put in the potentially embarrassing position of having to tell him that his fee is too high for your organization to afford. Find out, if he consents to come, how he will travel, if he wishes to be met, and whether or not he wants you to make a hotel reservation for him.

When your telephone conversation is successfully concluded and you have secured your speaker's consent to appear for you, end your call by telling him that you will immediately send him a letter confirming the exchange that has just taken place between you. And proceed to do exactly that, the following day at the latest, keeping a copy of it for your files.

In case you have never written a letter of confirmation, here is a sample:

"Mr. John Smith
15 Doe Street
Smithville, Connecticut (Zip Code)

Dear Mr. Smith:

As I promised, I am writing to you in confirmation of the telephone conversation I had with you yesterday, August 30, when you kindly consented to address the Blankville College Club. My understanding is that you will speak at our annual luncheon meeting next May 25, at 12 noon, in our Club rooms at 25 Sycamore Road.

We look forward to hearing you tell us about your latest book and how you came to write it.

As you requested, I am reserving a room at the Western Hotel for the night of May 24. I understand from our telephone conversation that your wife will be accompanying you, so we shall reserve accommodations accordingly.

I myself shall be at the airport to meet you when you arrive at 7:15 P.M., and shall be happy to drive you to your hotel and answer any questions you may have about our town or our Club.

If you require any special equipment, such as blackboard, projector, or tape recorder, will you please let us know as early as possible, so that we may have it ready for you.

I should also like to confirm the length of your talk: thirty minutes, with a fifteen-minute question period. There will be some seventy-five women in your audience, so it will be a fairly informal group. Also, since it is agreeable to you, we shall arrange for a television interview with our local news commentator.

We have noted that your fee is $200 plus travel and hotel expenses. Can you tell us in advance what these will be?

Will you please send us biographical material for my introduction and the publicity? May we also have two glossy photographs of yourself to send to our two newspapers?

We are most grateful to you for consenting to address our Club. It will be a privilege both to see and hear you on May 25.

With thanks and good wishes,

Sincerely yours,

Mary Jones, Program Chairman
Blankville College Club"

Please note that this letter contains the following important information:

the date, time and place of meeting,
the fee the speaker is to receive,
the number of people to expect in the audience,
the length of his talk, and that it will be followed by
    questions,
who will meet him,
location of the Club,
hotel accommodations,
arrangements for a television interview,
availability of all necessary equipment.

The important thing to bear in mind is that the speaker should be given well in advance, if possible in the letter of confirmation, all the information you can think of that will be helpful to him. For example, if your program follows a dinner, or if it takes place late in the evening, indicate in your note if dress is to be formal or informal. Women speakers especially appreciate receiving this information without having to ask for it.

If your speaker is to be part of a large program, one on which other speakers or performers will appear, tell him about the others, so that he will know exactly what to expect. If possible, let him know at what point in the program he will appear.

Having made your telephone contact and written a careful and detailed letter of confirmation, there is nothing to do now until the actual meeting date approaches. Then, a few weeks before the event, write to your speaker again, simply saying that your organization is expecting him and that you will meet him at the already appointed place and time.

Meantime, he may have written to you to tell you what special arrangements or equipment he needs, and in your note you can assure him that everything has been prepared according to his wishes.

Although a telephone call seems to be the most efficient approach to a speaker, many program chairmen prefer to make their approach by letter, and such a letter would contain substantially the same information as that put in the note of confirmation. If your speaker is a local person, a visit to issue the invitation may be in order. However, the manner of approach should rest upon circumstances and the good judgment of the program chairman.

If it is possible, have some idea of the quality of your speaker or performer before you invite him, either through having heard him yourself or through a report of someone whose judgment you trust. Large lecture bureaus* issue brochures with photographs of their speakers, describing them and their subjects. In these instances you may be sure that those so presented have been very carefully screened before their names are listed. The reputation and continued

---

* Some of these are listed in the Appendix.

success of the lecture bureau depend upon the reception of its speakers.

Between the time the program has been securely arranged and the actual day of the meeting, there will have been conferences by the chairmen of arrangements, publicity, hospitality, and whatever other committees have been involved in the plans. Even though the program chairman may not have any direct responsibility for the other matters, nevertheless she will want to know that everything is going to run smoothly when the day arrives.

Meantime, you as the program chairman carry out all the responsibilities you have assumed. At the time agreed upon, you meet the speaker and escort him and his wife to the hotel. You observe that they are tired from the trip, and you leave them as soon as they are registered and on their way to their room.

Before departing you ask them if you can be of any service to them in the morning, before the meeting. Invariably the speaker prefers a quiet few hours before his actual appearance, and you simply arrange either to call for him yourself or to have someone else do it, and transport him to the meeting. This is a courtesy which is actually only rarely extended to a speaker, and most of them find themselves on their own once they have reached their destination.

When your speaker arrives on the scene, make him feel welcome and introduce him to those who are present. Very likely he will be escorted to a room or an area where the guests at the head table are gathered. Be sure he is made comfortable and not left standing alone. Club members often stand in awe of a distinguished speaker, and sometimes diffidence makes them seem cool. Remember that the greatest are nearly always the kindest. A speaker is almost bound to have a warm and outgoing personality, and he usually appreciates being approached with enthusiasm.

Either the president of the organization will introduce the speaker, or this privilege will be assigned to the program chairman. No matter which one does it, the introduction should be carefully prepared and contain brief, pertinent, and above all, accurate information about the person being presented. Presumably he has replied to your request for biographical information about himself. Often prepared outlines contain more material than there is time to use, and the introducer must select with discretion those items which seem most appropriate. It is sometimes mistakenly thought that a lengthy introduction is a compliment to the speaker. Actually it is not, for it cuts down the time which has been allotted to him and puts the introducer in the limelight. Too protracted an introduction bores the audience. On the other hand, if it is too brief, the audience finds it equally annoying, so a careful course must be steered between Scylla and Charybdis.

At last the moment comes when the program is over, the speech has been given, the question period is ended, the fee has been paid with a check made out in advance and sealed in an envelope, and the chairman breathes a sigh of relief.

Frequently at this point the speaker departs, also breathing a sigh of relief. However, this is not always the case. If radio or television appearances have been arranged, someone in your organization takes responsibility for getting him to the station. Again this task customarily falls on the program chairman, either to do himself or to find someone who will do it for him.

Some organizations entertain for a performer either before or after his appearance. Many speakers enjoy being lionized, but there are those who avoid it if they can. An organization, or a hostess, should be guided by the preference of the guest.

Now, assuming that the speaker has departed, the only remaining task is writing your letter of thanks. This should be carefully thought out and worded so that it is directly relevant to the presentation that has been made. The notes of thanks mean a great deal to a speaker, and often he or his agent uses quotations from them in advertising brochures. Two sample letters follow:

"Mrs. W. D. G.
1000 Blank Blvd.
Blankville, Ohio (zip code)

Dear Mrs. G.:
    This is to tell you how very much we all enjoyed the biographical sketch of Cassie Chadwick which you gave to our Club on Tuesday afternoon.
    Your appearance in a gown actually worn by the 'Queen of the Cons,' your careful and thorough research, and your exciting presentation made the afternoon a truly memorable one for all of us. For some you vividly recalled an almost forgotten bit of the past.
    Your words were clear and easily audible throughout the room. Many of our members expressed appreciation for that, as well as admiration for your fluency.
    With many thanks and good wishes,

                    Sincerely yours,

                    Jane Doe, Program Chairman"

"Mrs. W. L. F.
3000 Blank Blvd.
Blankville, Ohio (zip code)

Dear Mrs. F.:
    Please accept our thanks for the beautiful program on Kashmir and Nepal which you gave for our Club on February 18.
    Your slides are exquisite and your commentary both informal and interesting. The fact that you made the trip while you were having difficulties with your eye both impressed and inspired your audience.
    It was good of you to give us your afternoon, and to bring your own equipment with you.
    Please remember us to your son John, who figured so pleasantly in your program.
    Thank you again.

                    Sincerely yours,

                    Jane Doe, Program Chairman"

    So far, attention has been given to the paid speaker or performer. Most organizations will be able to pay for their program only a few times during a year, and usually only once. For all the other months, or even weeks, the program chairman has the task of finding free talent.

The thoughtful chairman realizes that she really owes more to those who are willing to contribute their talents free than to those who are rewarded by a fee, often a fairly high one.

How can appreciation be shown to those who give rather than sell? First of all, by realizing what motivates them to do so. A good number give talks in order to keep their own names, or the names of enterprises for which they work, before the public. This is a quite common motivation. Recognizing this, every effort should be made to get suitable publicity of every kind for these speakers. List them in your program booklet; get notices in your newspapers; send announcements; post on your bulletin boards information about their forthcoming appearances.

Some people perform without charge because they can afford to do so, and because they sincerely love what they are doing. This may be especially true of those who are amateurs in the arts: music, the dance, or drama. In many communities commercial outlets do not exist for this group, and opportunities to use their God-given talents might be welcome.

There are some in the group of givers who are true philanthropists and earnestly wish to share some gift or experience which has meant much to them. Perhaps travelers are the best example of this genre. More and more of them are returning from the far reaches of the earth, bringing back excellent motion picture films and color slides. Many of these travelers love to share, and in doing so live again their own happy and colorful experiences.

There is a very small minority who finds in public appearance a great source of ego inflation. Every performer enjoys some of this, but beware of those who ask to be on your program—nay, who beg to be on it! These are invariably the ones who are thinking not of the pleasure they may give an audience, but rather of the glory which may accrue to themselves.

But when you have free talent of any kind on your program, a very special effort should be made to get good audiences for them. From the speaker's point of view there is no greater let-down than to come into a group of ten or twelve people, when he has been led to believe that he would be addressing fifty. A paid speaker has his fee, and although he may prefer a bigger audience, he can at least comfort himself with the thought that he has not appeared for naught.

Some organizations, even though they can not pay a fee, have the custom of giving their speaker a small gift as a token of their appreciation.

But whatever else may be done, a carefully composed and promptly dispatched letter of thanks should go to the free speaker, just as it does to the one to whom a fee is paid. Indeed, it is even more important that the former be rewarded with thoughtfully expressed gratitude and appreciation.

If the speaker is on the paid staff of any type of agency—cultural, industrial, governmental, or whatever—a letter of thanks should go to the head of that agency. It is appreciated both by the speaker and by the administrator to whom he is responsible. This courtesy should be observed most especially if the provision of speakers is a policy of the agency.

Such a letter might read like this:

"Dr., John H. Smith
Superintendent of Schools
Blankville, Ohio (zip code)

Dear Dr. Smith:
    Yesterday afternoon we had the great pleasure of observing *A Children's Dance Festival*, given to us by the students of your Elementary School, led by Miss Helen Green.
    They performed for our Golden Age Club. Their vitality and youthful enjoyment of what they were doing delighted all of us and gave us one of the happiest afternoons we have ever had.

The children were charming to the older people, and completely won their hearts.

We are grateful to you and to Miss Green for making this experience possible.

Sincerely yours,

Jane Doe, Program Chairman"

The writer of such a note may be surprised to receive a most gracious reply from the person addressed, indicating that this expression of gratitude is an encouragement to continue a service whose usefulness had been questioned.

One can never err in voicing feelings of appreciation.

5

GETTING THE AUDIENCE

"Attracting a crowd" becomes a major objective with any group which presents programs, whether it be a small club, a major cultural agency, or an important business concern. Too often sight of the real reasons for having programs is lost in the scramble to assemble an impressive audience. The real reasons should never be forgotten, and we should think in terms something like the following:

"In October we are celebrating United Nations Day. This is a great milestone in world history, and it deserves all the attention we are giving it. We have engaged an outstanding speaker to help us in our observance, and in doing so we have discharged part of our resposibility. We have just as much responsibility—and possibly more—in getting our speaker's message to as many of our compatriots as may be reached, not because we want a hall full to overflowing of paying guests, but because what he has to say is important and will help us better to understand the times in which we are living." In other words, we should be at least lightly touched with a sense of mission. If we are, the mechanics of attracting an audience become less perfunctory.

There are numerous techniques by which people may be informed of coming programs:

    I. Many agencies—clubs and others—publish a program book or something similar. Usually the dates therein cover events for an entire year, but this is not always the case.

Ordinarily the yearbooks contain a list of officers and committees, as well as any special rules the organization may wish to call to the attention of the members. For example, in one club where the programs are presented in the form of written papers, the yearbook clearly states that no paper should consume more than fifteen minutes in the reading.

The most important portion of these booklets from this chapter's point of view is the part which lists the program: subjects, speakers, dates, times, places, which of the meetings are for members only and which are open to the general public.

This little publication is certainly a basic means of reaching an audience, and may go to groups ranging in size from a few dozen to literally thousands.

Whoever has been assigned the duty of compiling this tool (often it is the program chairman again) should do so with the greatest care. Printing is costly and must be accomplished within a budget allowance. Outward attractiveness has something to do with the kind of attention it will command, and painstaking thought should be given to paper, cover design, and print type. Be as sure that all pertinent information is on the cover as you are that accurate data are on the inside. The person responsible should do the proof-reading himself and not leave the task to the printer.

In your estimate of quantity to be ordered allow for several to be deposited with your public library and a supply to be kept on hand for possible new members.

Incidentally, many libraries keep files of these programs, and looking through them may give you new ideas for your own.

Although an annual program schedule is the one most ordinarily compiled, especially by smaller groups, it is certainly not the only kind. A good example of a calendar of events issued quarterly is that of Cleveland's Live Long and Like It Library Club. The program continues throughout the year, without any seasonal lull, and the announcements for it are issued every three months, coinciding with the four seasons, with the covers designed to symbolize the time of year.

Some program announcements are issued monthly, others bimonthly, semimonthly, or weekly. The pattern is established to fit the circumstances. The most noteworthy thing about these bulletins is that they are received by a certain definite membership, and that these people and no others are the ones who get this particular information.

II. Newspapers and Other Mass Media.

The newspapers are generally the first thought of those who have the responsibility for getting out the word about a forthcoming event. This is logical, for the majority of our population subscribes to at least one newspaper per family.

While the program chairmen and their committees are usually responsible for the printed announcements emanating from an organization to its members, it is invariably the publicity, or public relations, committee which is charged with getting information into the mass media: newspapers, radio, and television.

The desirable characteristics of a program chairman were listed in a previous chapter. The appointing officer should be equally careful in the selection of a publicity chairman. Generally the requirements of the latter would be these:

A warm and outgoing personality capable of establishing instant contact.

Some sense of what is newsworthy.

An ability to be always courteous and cooperative in relation to those members of the press who handle the news to be offered.

A certain detachment and willingness to be self-effacing in favor of giving the limelight to others.

Some ability to write, a knowledge of how to prepare a release. and the realization that brevity is the soul of wit.

A telephoned piece of information, unless it is overwhelmingly sensational, will most likely be ignored.

Know the setup of the newspapers. Certain items would be sent to a club editor, others to the city editor, and still others to the society editor.

The person who is in charge of publicity should learn how it should be prepared. It should be typed and follow the old formula of telling with complete accuracy who, what, when, where, why and how. Material should be presented in good form with appropriate photographs accompanying the copy. Because of local interest, some newspapers choose to publish photographs of the local chairman or committee, either instead of, or in addition to, that of the performer. Spelling of names should be carefully checked, and such courtesies should be observed as these:

Never use initials for unmarried women.

Never use only one initial. Where only one is known, use the full name.

Use Mrs. or Miss preceding women's names, unless specifically requested to do otherwise.

Omit the Mr. in writing of men when you use first names or initials.

If your speaker has a special title, get it from him in its correct form.

Heed deadlines which have been given you for submitting copy.

These suggestions relative to newspaper publicity are equally applicable to radio and television.

If an event is of sufficient importance, it may receive notice on a news broadcast, or be given its own spot announcement. Interesting speakers may be presented to a listening or viewing audience in special interviews. Just as it is necessary to establish contacts with the appropriate personnel on the newspaper, so it is equally important to become acquainted with the news staff of the television and radio stations.

III. Mailings.

The first question that arises in connection with the mailing of announcements is usually: to whom should they go?

Naturally they would go first of all to an organization's entire membership, even though an announcement of the occasion may have been already made.

Beyond that, if the sponsoring body wishes to have a large turnout, a correspondingly large mailing list will have to be used.

Creating a mailing list takes great skill, patience, and ingenuity, and not every organization can produce someone with these qualities. However, when such a person is available, he or she should be given the task of compiling a mailing list of individuals and institutions which could be used whenever the need arose.

How does one go about producing such a list? Again, your public library should be a prime resource for this kind of information. If it keeps on file the yearbooks or other publications which are issued by local organizations, you have at your fingertips names both of individuals and of groups that might have an interest in your offering. The Chamber of Commerce usually keeps data on local businesses and industries and their affiliates. If a Chamber of Commerce is actively concerned with the community as a whole, it is likely to have files on other types of local clubs and groups.

Labor unions have become increasingly alert to activities beyond their own narrow fields. Many of them have educational directors, and some, like the United Auto Workers and the International Machinists Association, carry on outstanding programs. Their representatives often welcome involvement in community affairs and may be willing to add to your list the names of their own interested officers and members.

Every community has its religious agencies, mainly Catholic, Jewish, and Protestant. Some of them will lend their membership lists; others, for ethical reasons, will not. Some will cooperate to the extent of enclosing your notice with a mailing of their own.

Telephone books, especially the yellow pages, provide another possibility for building a mailing list. They give the names of doctors, attorneys, photographers, and other professional people, as well as schools, churches, and social agencies. Mailings may be addressed to the latter, although it is doubtful that such impersonal communications receive the attention they should.

The newspapers have been mentioned as a source of program pointers. An assiduous clipper can glean excellent additions to a mailing list by daily examination of club and society news.

If a Blue Book or Social Register is available, this document would supply valuable information on those who might be favorably inclined to attend certain types of programs.

In addition to the ingenuity and patience mentioned at the outset, persistence is a requisite in the compilation of a mailing list, for the list must not only be assembled but also kept up to date.

There is an easy access to mailing lists, but like most easy ways it is expensive. Many different kinds may be purchased, and a good public relations or advertising agency will tell you how to go about this.

Getting the list is only part of the mailing technique. The announcement must be composed and then reproduced by one of the many processes available.

Again, wording an announcement or invitation temptingly and titillatingly is an art, and your organization is fortunate if it has on its rolls someone who has this talent.

The communication may be fashioned anywhere from the extremely formal to the equally informal. But whatever the approach, the basic information must be there: subject of the meeting; name of the guest speaker and an introductory sentence or two about him; details of date, time, place, and tickets; price; why the meeting is being held, and all other pertinent facts.

Some groups send out a "Dear Friend" type of letter, others send a flier, and still others a very formal paneled card. It is difficult to say which of these approaches is the most successful.

Whatever the form, a first-class envelope mailing wins more consideration than a bulk-mailed piece or a post card. Too many busy people have the bad habit of tossing third-class envelopes into the waste basket automatically without opening them.

Timing is essential. If the information goes out too far in advance, it is likely to be put aside and forgotten, and if it is too late, those to whom it is addressed may already have engagements.

Some groups mail two notifications, the first one intended to arouse curiosity, and the second containing definite information.

For a rule of thumb, two to three weeks ahead of a function should be adequate notice.

IV. The Telephone.

In all likelihood the most effective means of reaching and interesting an audience is the telephone.

Special committees are sometimes appointed, whose sole task is to telephone information about meetings to members, and when called for, to non-members.

There is something personal and direct about a telephone call, and this attention pleases most people. At the same time, there is a minority that resents what is regarded as an intrusion into privacy.

Anyone who has executed a telephone assignment quickly realizes that in many cases his conversations are going to involve more than the simple giving of information about a coming event. He will discover that he is to become the recipient of much unexpected intelligence: reasons why his interlocutor has not been able to come to meetings, hitherto repressed complaints about the programs or the administration. These calls frequently result in bringing a lost sheep back into the fold.

The chief weakness of this approach is that people are too likely to promise over the wire that they will attend, but unless they are actually pinned down to taking a ticket in advance, may fail to appear at the event.

However, the fact remains that it is much easier to arouse interest with a telephone call than with a mailing piece, but perhaps both methods should be employed if prospects for good attendance seem dim.

In using the telephone bear these points in mind:

1. Have your list well prepared, with correct telephone numbers attached to the names.

2. Do not skip anyone, even though you feel sure that he may not be a good prospect.

3. Have all the facts well in mind, including those that would go in a mailed announcement.

4. Regard your assignment as a pleasure and not as a burdensome task to be discharged as quickly as possible. Allow yourself plenty of time for each conversation.

5. Follow up immediately on anything you promise on the telephone.

V. Tables.

One method which has been used successfully at programs involving meals is the selling of entire tables rather than only individual tickets.

Organizations with large staffs or memberships who attend these functions often like this group seating. As an added inducement the name of the organization is placed prominently on the table.

This practice has pros and cons: while it is easier and more comfortable for a homogeneous group to cluster together, an opportunity is missed to enlarge acquaintanceship and to exchange ideas with strangers.

Somewhat associated with this approach is one which has been becoming more prevalent in recent years. Before major events some hosts and hostesses give dinner parties from which the guests proceed in a body to a lecture, concert, play, or whatever program awaits them.

For a neophyte in presenting programs there is bound to be a surprise at the amount of work required to attract an audience. It is only natural to believe that if an entertaining and worthwhile program is prepared, people will flock to it. This once was true, but in these days of keen competitive bidding for every moment of the day, it is, alas, no longer so.

Some areas, aware of this competition, have established a calendar service so that dates may be cleared before being set, and duplication avoided. This may be effective in a smaller community, but unless there is universal cooperation by those who plan meetings, the system quickly breaks down.

6

THE PREPARATIONS

Some of the synonyms which the dictionary lists for *preparation* are: precaution, rehearsal, provision, forethought, prior measure, foresight, prudence, timely care, and a few others. Preparations for a meeting include all of these, and more.

Previous chapters have dealt with the specific subjects of planning the program, securing the speaker, and attracting an audience. These are the first steps, the outlines on the canvas which must be filled in. This phase of our topic has many facets of which inexperienced planners are not aware. Some of them are so minute and obscure that no one thinks of them until an affair is ruined because of the neglect of just one of them. Do you remember the line that some of us learned in grade school, "Because of a nail the battle was lost?" That is the kind of detail we have in mind.

The main responsibility for physical preparations falls on the Chairman and members of the Arrangements Committee, working closely, as all committees do, with the head of the organization.

The Chairman of this Committee should have these characteristics:

> The ability to prevision the appearance of the room or platform.
> A systematic and orderly mind that can catalog in advance all requirements for the function.
> The capacity to work well with different kinds of people, often under last-minute tension. This includes not only

fellow club members but also workmen in the meeting places (waiters or waitresses, projectionists, exhibitors).

A temperament which remains cool and balanced even when things are not going according to previous plans.

A willingness to do some physical work if it becomes necessary. How many chairs and tables have been moved around by members of arrangements committees!

When this Committee starts its work it already knows what kind of meeting is going to be held and approximately how large an attendance is expected. It is possible that the meeting place has already been determined. This would certainly be true if the organization has its own club house or its own rooms. If this is not the case, however, the Arrangements Committee may well be involved in the selection of location.

This choice will be made with the following points in mind:

Location. This should be as central as possible, in consideration of the convenience of those who will be converging upon it from all directions. Its nearness to public transportation and to parking areas are other factors which sometimes should be taken into account.

Size. It should be large enough to accommodate comfortably the number expected. If your program involves the use of more than one room, be sure that each one is suitable as nearly as possible to the needs of the projected meetings, bearing in mind that sometimes compromise is necessary and that the wind occasionally must be tempered to the shorn lamb.

Relationships. If a very large and complex function, such as a convention, is being planned, the Arrangements Committee must be careful to use a number of local facilities without seeming to favor any special one of them.

With the location of the forthcoming meeting assured, the Arrangements Committee now concentrates on the physical setup. This process can begin very early both as far as planning and taking certain definite steps are concerned. A most essential first step is to become well acquainted with the scene of the forthcoming meeting. If it is to be held in a place where a special person is in charge of rooms—a hotel manager, for example, or a public relations officer—an early conference with that person would be very much in order.

Such a conference will yield the information you need, and will give you the opportunity to let your own requirements be known at an early date. It is well to follow such a conference with a letter of confirmation (with a copy kept for your files) detailing the agreements which have been reached. Such a letter protects you in case your instructions were not understood. No one can say, "But this is how you told me to do it!" if you have a copy of the letter giving detailed directions which have not been followed.

If a meeting is held in an organization's own quarters, of course this preliminary is unnecessary.

If, however, it is the kind—which many are—to be held in a private home, an informal conference with the host or hostess would not be amiss, especially if an outside speaker is to be brought in. In this situation it is rare for the comfort of the speaker to be carefully considered. Frequently when he has notes or books to which he wishes to refer, there is nothing provided on which he can place them. The poor speaker is constrained to crouch over a coffee table, or lean in what he hopes is a nonchalant manner against a grand piano or its equivalent. Lighting, too, may leave something to be desired. Many a speaker realizes that if he voices his needs on the scene he may cause an embarrassed flurry, and so does the best he can. The result may take one of two directions: he will never again accept a speaking engagement that will place him in such a position, or next time he will make known his requirements well in advance. An alert Arrangements Chairman can prevent these difficulties by ascertaining the speaker's needs and tactfully relaying them to the host or hostess at whose home the meeting is scheduled.

In planning the physical arrangements of a meeting, no matter where, and no matter how large, the same essentials should be kept in mind:

> If registration or payment of a fee is required, be prepared for this. Have sufficient table space available, pre-

ferably outside the meeting area itself, with a good crew manning the tables. When a large crowd is expected, either to register or pay for tickets, it is a good idea to indicate divisions of the alphabet on easily seen cards, and have the influx of people systematically divided according to the initials of their last names. Unless something like this is done, the result can be chaos and bedlam.

In addition to those at the tables it is well to have at least one other person explaining the system to the guests and helping them to get into the proper lines.

As far as arrangements in the meeting place itself are concerned the comfort of both performer and audience should take priority.

Try to arrange for an entrance behind the audience, so that late comers will not distract attention.

In the same connection, do your best to fill the front seats first and prevent, if you can, the inevitable crowding to the rear. Especially at a meal function it is disconcerting for the speaker to see large blanks in the front row.

Try to persuade the guests to move in towards the center of a row, so that those who come later do not have to climb over feet and squeeze in front of knees.

Be sure that the lighting is good. If there are windows in the room—a rarity in these days of air conditioning and artificial light—try to seat your audience and speaker so that they do not face a glare.

If there is a platform, use it, even though it may seem formal to do so. The audience likes to have a clear view of the program, and they have a right to expect it.

This next may be considered a matter of preference, but it is rather a nice touch if the chairman seats himself in the audience after the speaker has been introduced. In that way attention may be focussed where it belongs—on the very reason why the meeting is being held.

See that the room is well ventilated. It is impossible to prohibit smoking nowadays, and the practice must be lived with. Supply sufficient ash trays so that there is a minimum fire hazard. If the meeting is held in a building where smoking is prohibited by law, provide signs to that effect, or have ushers who will courteously inform the guests of the rule.

Make sure that there are adequate facilities for checking or for hanging clothes. This is especially essential during bad weather and at very large meetings.

Pay special attention to the acoustics. If it is necessary

to use a microphone, test it well in advance to make sure that it works and that it will not produce strange noises at the most inopportune times.

When you are making your initial choice of room, try to select a quiet one, away from intruding street noises. Some of the internal noises you cannot foresee, such as clanking of radiators and the clatter of dishwashing. For such contingences it is well to have a predesignated trouble-shooter who will rush to remedy such situations the minute they arise.

Your foresight will also tell you not to take a room with pillars. If you simply have no other choice, arrange your seating so that the pillars do not interfere with visibility. Otherwise, some of your guests will never again come to anything you have a finger in arranging.

Check on washroom facilities, especially if you are arranging a function involving large numbers of people. This may seem a prosaic and even unimportant item, but it is not. It has happened that at the very last minute before a big meeting the discovery was made that all washroom facilities on the floor were locked up, and what a flurry that caused!

If your performers will need to change into costumes, provide an area which may be used as dressing rooms.

The program chairman has checked with the speaker in advance and presumably has passed on the list of his needs. If the list calls for the bringing in to your meeting place any kind of extra labor, check union regulations in force there. This is particularly applicable if the plan includes any kind of film projecting. Otherwise have all the items required by the speaker conveniently at hand and in good working order. If he has asked for a blackboard, don't forget the chalk. Have a pointer available. If visual aids are used, it will undoubtedly be needed.

We have all seen speakers remove their wrist watches and place them on the lectern or table (and then sometimes forget to look at them!), but for the convenience of your performer it is well to have a clock plainly visible.

Should your program include the distribution of any kind of material, have enough people ready to do this. Even if this distribution is not in the advance planning, it is still a good idea to have in reserve a few workers who could spring into the breach should the speaker unexpectedly present you with an armful of sheets he would like the audience to have.

If you display the flag, be sure that you have it done correctly.* If the flags of one or more countries are displayed, it is vital to know the position in which they should be placed relative to Old Glory.

Many programs include music either as an integral part of the proceedings or as background. It would seem superfluous to say be sure a piano is placed at the right spot for the musician, but it has happened from time to time that a piano was nowhere in sight when the time came for music.

Your floral decorations, if you have them, should of course be considered and ordered well in advance. These are very important in setting the tone of the meeting, especially if it is a large one and is of the banquet type. The desirability of working closely with the personnel in charge of physical arrangements at the meeting place was mentioned earlier, and in planning your decorations this group can be of inestimable assistance in counseling you as well as in supplying your needs. Color of table linen and of the skirt to be placed around the head table; whether or not to use candelabra; type of glassware—on all these and other matters a maitre d'hotel and his staff—or his equivalent in other places —will give you a helping hand. How elaborate your decorations can be depends of course on your budget. But whether the budget is large, small or even non-existent, the creative and ingenious person will find this part of preparing for the meeting the most fun of all.

Reference has frequently been made to meal functions. Responsibility for these may fall on the Arrangements Committee, or a special committee may have been appointed to assume this one duty.

But however it is handled, this again is an assignment with which you will need the help of the staff connected with your meeting place. Again, seek them out at the earliest

---

* Basic rules for display of the flag appear in Appendix.

possible moment and discuss your menu with them, whether it be for breakfast, luncheon, tea or cocktails, or dinner. Budget limitations will enter into your planning here too, and make known at once what these are. Larger hotels are usually prepared with a variety of preplanned menus at different prices. Less formally organized places, such as department store tea rooms or restaurants, will give you this information orally.

The good planner will not order a menu perfunctorily, but will take a number of things into consideration. If the occasion falls on a Friday, either order fish for everyone, or supply fish as a choice; if you expect a large attendance of Jewish people, do not order pork or ham; if your audience is going to be mainly women, select something light, particularly if the occasion is a luncheon; if many of your group are likely to be older people, have something that is easy to chew, and nothing with nuts or little seeds, remembering the limitations of dentures.

Negotiations concerning meals are again something which should always be confirmed with a letter to the person with whom you are dealing.

Also, connected with this type of function is the matter of guarantee. A few days before the occasion takes place, it is quite properly expected that a firm guarantee of attendance will be given, so that the correct amounts of food may be ordered. Some places will allow a reasonable leeway in this matter, but some expect a precise count, to the last one. Some wary chairmen give a final count of a few less than are actually expected, knowing from experience that not everyone who reserved a ticket, or even who paid for one, will appear. However, they are taking a chance in doing this. But no matter how you handle it, the important thing to remember is that you are responsible for the guarantee you have made.

This brings up the matter of refunds if tickets are not used, or responsibility for payment if a ticket is reserved and not picked up. Some organizations are lenient in both regards; some take into account extenuating circumstances, such as illess or accident; others are very strict, will not refund paid tickets, and will hold accountable those who promised to pick up and pay at the door for tickets and then did not do so.

All this raises the whole question of whether or not tickets are necessary, and again, it depends both on the event and on the workers responsible for both planning and funds.

In one specific institution we have in mind, those who belong to it are likely to misplace their tickets. So none are used. A very careful system of collecting money ahead of time is employed, and equally careful records are kept of those who paid. Prepared for them well in advance, to be distributed on the day of the affair, are envelopes with names typed at the top and filed in alphabetical order, filled with programs, name tags ready to be pinned on, and any other material to be given out. The name tags act as tickets of admission to all sessions.

If tickets for meals are used, they should be numbered. This numbering may be done by the printer, or it may be done by hand. Those sold should be listed in numerical order, with the name of the purchaser recorded for each. This is a good way to avoid chaos.

Mention has been made of the device of selling entire tables to groups if a meal function is involved. If this is done, it is a good idea to divide the entire supply of tickets into packs of eight, ten, twelve, or whatever the seating capacity of the tables may be. The person in charge of this phase of preparations should study the arrangements of the dining area and construct a work chart.* As each table is purchased, the name of the group should be recorded on the chart. Many hotels and larger establishments will supply a printed chart of their table placement. In addition to this graphic record, it is advisable to make a separate numerical list of the tables, and enter on it all payments as received. Thus you will have at all times an up-to-date picture of space sold, payments made and amounts still outstanding.

---

* See Appendix for sample chart.

To facilitate seating, each table will have on it both its number and the name of the group for whom it is being held.

Name tags have been mentioned as an admission device instead of tickets. Many large meetings, notably conventions, employ this method of identifying those who are eligible to attend their sessions. Stationers have available a great variety of these tags. Currently the most popular are those with an adhesive on the back, which allow them to be fastened to a garment without pins.

Each chairman in charge of arrangements should keep in mind the helpfulness of making a checklist of things that must be done before a meeting gets under way. Such a list will vary according to the type and circumstances of the meeting. Here is a suggested one:

Check: Seating arrangements and numbers, with chart
      Speakers' table and place cards (if it is a meal
        function)
      Chairs and lectern on platform
      Water for the speaker
      Pointer
      Signaler for slide changes
      Blackboard and chalk
      Electric outlet for slide projector
      Microphones (test them)
      Flag on platform to right of speaker
      Switches for extinguishing all room lights, for slide
        showing (This would be true of any projecting.
        Slides are mentioned only as a specific example.)
      Pencils and paper for question period
      Piano

As the chairman makes sure that each item has been attended to, it may be crossed out.

It is sad but true that the experienced arranger of meetings eventually learns that no matter how many details have been thought of in advance, there is almost always an elusive one that rears its ugly head at the last moment.

7

THE EXTRA TOUCHES

Seasoned meeting planners will think of many embellishments which, although they are not essential, will increase the enjoyment of members and guests.

Displays and exhibits are one example of an extra touch which may serve several purposes. In the first place, a thoughtfully prepared exhibit on the subject of your meeting adds at least two more dimensions to it—the visual and the tactile.

Such an exhibit may be one or more of the following:

Books on the subject. These may be supplied either by your public library or by one of your book stores, sometimes by both. Some libraries furnish not only books for display, but make it possible for those interested to borrow them on the spot. Also, some of them supply colorful posters to go along with the books, announcing programs or telling of available library services. In addition your library may provide you with book lists relating to your subject, to be picked up by your guests as they browse among the books.

It is quite common in some areas for book stores to allow their wares to go out on consignment, in care of a responsible person, and to permit that person to sell them.

Mention was made earlier of Book and Author luncheons. It would be a slight to the authors involved if their writings were not on display either in or very near the meeting room.

In this category of book displays we might include other types of printed materials, such as pamphlets or fliers. These are available in quantities, depending, of course, on your subject.

travel and fashion supplied an exhibit of costumes which she had collected in the many countries she had visited. Similarly, another traveler offered a fan collection.

An industrialist whose hobbies are traveling, photography, and collecting Judaica lent a beautiful display of ceremonial and folk art pieces when he gave an illustrated lecture on his travels to Israel.

Displays like these may range from the simplest to the most elaborate, depending upon time, resources and space available.

Programs on flower arranging, hobbies, and handicraft almost cry aloud for visual supplementing. All the collecting hobbies lend themselves perfectly to display: stamps, coins, buttons—there is no end to them.

Pictures alone can make an effective exhibit. Nowadays too, a variety of visual devices have been perfected to make possible the continuous showing of slides or film strips which tell a story of process, accomplishment, or experience. Local suppliers of audiovisual equipment will tell you about these, and sometimes arrangements can be made to rent them.

Aside from adding the visual and tactile dimensions already referred to, these exhibits serve two other purposes. First, they give people something to do while they are waiting for the meeting to begin. Second, they may be a means of helping a shy or lonely person to be more relaxed, and they may possibly even be a means of helping him to forget his shyness. Third, they may be an avenue leading to a new interest. More than one person has started a collection of something after seeing a good one displayed, and many a stay-at-home has ventured on journeys after picking up the right book or travel folder in a display.

Mention has been made of soft music during a meal function. This is a rather common extra touch. Going one step further, some organizations play unobtrusive recorded music before a meeting begins, so that the early comers may spend the time pleasantly while waiting for the chairman to call the meeting to order.

While following rules of procedure to the letter, it is

THE EXTRA TOUCHES

Especially in the health field there is a wealth of pic display pieces. Arthritis Foundations, Cancer Soci Diabetes Associations, Anti-Tuberculosis Leagues, all their stories to be known, and practically all of them willing to disseminate their health education informa Not only do they have fliers and brochures, but ofter teresting stand-up exhibits as well.

Some United States governmental agencies, such as Pure Food and Drug Administration, have materials free distribution. If the agency has an office in your to a call to them will yield the information you need. Tl agencies are listed in your telephone book under *U.S. C ernment, Health, Education, and Welfare.* Should they be represented in your community, your Congressman usually more than willing to be helpful in these matters

Some industries issue informative pieces (which, h ever, may not always be free) about their products a related items.

One is constantly surprised at the abundance of mater which exists for the asking—if one only knows where ask, or is willing to go to a little trouble to find out.

Objects or pictures. These can make most interesti displays either by themselves or, ideally, combined wi books.

A few examples of this type of exhibit will illustra how a meeting may be enhanced by including extra touche

For a series of programs on science a local scientil school lent apparatus to display.

One of the programs had to do with investigatioi which were currently going on under water, and a depar ment store lent a mannequin dressed in a diving suit.

A lecturer who was speaking on his camping trip i Europe asked if he could pitch his tent in the auditoriun where he was lecturing, so that his listeners would get more realistic idea of his experience. He did this, anc the bright blue and orange tent delighted the audienc as no description of it could have.

With a lecture on Negro contributions to American history and culture an exhibit of appropriate photographs was attached to the walls of the auditorium.

A speaker who had a lifelong interest in boating furnished a fascinating display of photographs, pennants and other marine paraphernalia which attracted almost more interest than his talk.

A woman lecturer who had a deep interest in both

still possible to do so with a flourish, and it is nearly always that little extra which gives distinction to a meeting and keeps it from being run-of-the-mill. The thought, not only of a corsage for the woman speaker, but one which matches her outfit; the care with which places are arranged so that table partners are congenial; color schemes that never clash; thoughtful extensions of your theme with displays or other devices of your own fashioning; the careful creation, if possible, of an atmosphere of harmony, tranquility, and high interest—all the things which are not absolutely essential to the routine success of a meeting, but which raise it from mediocrity to excellence—these are the extra touches which you create yourself out of your own wish and your own involvement. A book can only point the way, but you yourself do it.

8

PRESENTING THE SUBJECT

So far reference has been made chiefly to one type of program, the commonest one. That is the one in which a single speaker or performer communicates what he has to say or do, to an audience, large or small, which absorbs information or entertainment passively.

Those who seriously assume responsibility in any type of organization which presents programs either regularly or occasionally should certainly have in mind the various methods by which information may be communicated, as well as certain techniques that jolt the audience out of a merely passive role. Some of these will be listed and described:

The Lecture.

This, as has been said, is the most common and indeed, the easiest to arrange. It means the complete reliance on the skill of one person to interest, inform, and/or amuse an audience. If that one person is superlative, nothing can be more delightful than this kind of program. If he is mediocre or less, nothing can be more deadly. Lecturing is a business in our country, and it certainly flourishes today.

Following a lecture there may be a question period which eliminates the passivity* of the audience. This period may be conducted by the chairman or the questions fielded by the speaker. Sometimes the distribution of paper and pencils to the audience, with questions

---

* I have never understood why "audience passivity" is often referred to derogatorily. What is wrong with the silent absorption of something good?

then sifted and handed to the speaker, is a system that has proved quite satisfactory and should avoid the lengthy and involved circumlocutions which are hazards of oral questioning.

There are organizations that resort to question-planting, having a few members ready to spring questions the minute they are called for, in order to circumvent temporary—or even permanent—awkward lulls. This practice is condemned by some, but actually it is no more than innocent pump-priming. There is a growing feeling among program planners that question periods could be eliminated altogether, that they are useless unless they can be part of a more intensive discussion and exchange between speaker and audience.

The Debate.

Of course this is the formal presenting of two sides of a formally stated ("Resolved that," etc.) controversial question.

It would seem that the great days of the debate as a popular method of informing and stimulating an audience are gone. Perhaps radio and television are responsible for this, as they are for so many other changes of interest. In any event, it is many years since great debates have taken place on local platforms. On the floors of Congress, the United Nations, NATO or SEATO, yes, but no longer for the edification of the Gopher Prairie Women's Clubs.

There are still college debating teams, to be sure, and occasionally one has the opportunity to present them for a program, but not often enough even to take this resource into consideration.

This is regrettable, for the problems of our time are suited to good debate.

Platform arrangements would include tables on opposite sides of the stage, with chairs for the opponents. The chairman of the meeting would be seated in the center, with a lectern and microphone both for him and for the debaters who make their presentations on their feet. They are seated at the tables to facilitate their making notes in preparation for the rebuttals.

The Symposium.

With this method, several speakers each give a brief (usually limited to fifteen minutes) presentation of the aspect of a given subject with which they are most familiar.

This technique is especially valuable if the audience stands in a learning relationship to the speakers, and if experience is being drawn upon by the latter.

Social workers and educators employ this formula quite regularly, since it is an efficient way of communicating information and practical directions.

It is also conceivably a means of conveying ideas or points of view. However, as soon as these are presented, there should be opportunity for discussion, and symposia are not set up specifically for that. In fact, when discussion of that type begins, the symposium becomes

The Panel.

Like the symposium, this method requires the participation of several people, ideally five or six, although some advocates of the panel recommend as many as twelve.

Essentially a panel is simply a small discussion group discoursing in the presence of an audience. The subject may be one which has been assigned well in advance, or it may follow spontaneously the presentation of a subject by a specialist.

Presumably the panelists too are specialists in the topic they are discussing, which should be controversial, and members of the panel should hold divergent views on it. Too much consensus makes for a very dull panel indeed.

Unlike the symposium, where the participants are prepared to give a statement of a stipulated length, discussion on a panel is impromptu, and long discussions are taboo.

In both symposium and panel there is a chairman or moderator who introduces the speakers. Much more skill is required of the moderator of a panel, for his task is to keep the ball of discussion bouncing back and forth, to act as a referee, and to sum up what emerges from the whole procedure.

The objective of the panel is to stimulate thought, not to arrive at conclusions or decisions. Like beauty in the eyes of the beholder, they are in the mind of the listener.

If general audience participation is desired, a panel is an ideal intermediary step to achieving it, for in listening to the panel the audience is likely to become so involved mentally and emotionally that it is bursting to participate.

There was a time not long ago when the panel, like the debate, was a much more popular technique than it is today. Nowadays we are more likely than not to associate it with what goes on in television under the names of *What's My Line?*, *I've Got a Secret*, etc. Stage arrangements for the symposium and the panel are similar. The group is seated at a table which should be large enough to provide adequate room for all. Microphones and water should be within easy reach. The table should be skirted, especially if the panel includes women.

The Seminar.

In many ways this is close kin to the lecture, in that one person, a teacher or leader, gives instruction to a group on one subject, and answers their questions. The group is usually limited in size and is purposely kept small. This is an ideal method for intensive learning.

The Workshop or Institute.

This is invariably of longer duration than any of the methods so far listed, and may last for several days or even weeks.

The objective of a workshop is instruction or problem-solving. Workshops in human relations, for example, have been presented all over the country in the last few years.

Every technique of transmitting information and ideas is usually put to use in a workshop, from lecture to small discussion group, to role playing* and every medium, print, film, recordings, the spoken word, freely used.

The Clinic.

This is so similar to the workshop that all that need be said is that it involves a smaller number of people and that it is more highly concentrated on one subject.

The Conference.

Like the two just listed, this one may last for a longer period of time. In differentiating it from the other two, it may be pointed out that it usually involves more people, and although they have general interests in common, their chief concern is with a specialized facet.

---

* Role playing is the spontaneous acting out of the subject or question being considered by the group.

The best examples of the Conference are those held by members of a profession, where they come together under the large umbrella of that profession, but proceed as individuals to concentrate on the special phase in which their own competencies lie.

The Convention.

This is really all the others rolled into one, and any adequate treatment of this phenomenon, which has come to blossom in our time, would need a volume* all to itself.

Suffice it to say that it resembles a conference, in that it brings together those who have a common interest, and not necessarily a professional or working concern. Large national clubs, labor unions, professional organizations, and of course political bodies hold conventions.

They employ every technique, every skill, every resource that we have mentioned. In fact, they may be regarded as the epitome of the meeting, the end product of the process which started eons ago when man first woke up to the realization that two heads are better than one.

Attendance at conventions runs into the thousands, and they have become a big industry. Cities vie with one another in their efforts to attract them, and dates for large ones are set years in advance.

Planning for them is on a correspondingly grandiose scale with local committees paralleling national committees and carrying out all the necessary details of physical arrangements.

Only a few metropolises have facilities adequate for handling such a convention, and only a small number of us have more than one opportunity in a lifetime to be involved in planning even a portion of these Behemoths of the meeting world.

---

* *How to Plan, Produce and Publicize Special Events,* by Hal Golden and Kitty Hanson. N. Y., Oceana Publications, Inc. 1960.

9

THE SPEAKERS' TABLE

The speakers' table (or head table) is a very important part of any meal function, and it should not be treated casually by those who plan such affairs.

It may be a long table placed at one end of the room either at floor level or on a raised platform. The latter is preferable, because guests are interested in seeing not only the speakers but also the others who surround them. For informal affairs the head table may be simply one of the several at which all other guests are seated. It may be distinguished from the others by special decorations and, of course, by place cards.

There are a number of points to be taken into consideration when the speakers' table is being planned. Probably the first to be borne in mind is the fact that this table—its position in the room, its size, and those seated at it—represent a means of honoring your speakers, those invited to sit with them, and guests attending the function. If this is never forgotten, planning becomes easier.

The person who takes chief responsibility for the speakers' table is the president or head of an organization. Sometimes he will delegate this task to the program chairman or even, in the case of very large and important functions, will appoint a special committee charged with the sole duty of arranging the head table—that is, selecting the prospective guests, issuing invitations, making the seating chart, preparing the place cards, lining up the guests and getting them to their appointed places.

The location of the head table is usually determined by the room in which a luncheon or dinner is being held. Often there is a built-in platform, and the table can be placed nowhere else.

After learning how many may be seated at the table available in the place of meeting, the chairman determines how many guests should be included. Some organizations set an arbitrary number and say that there are to be no more than, for example, twelve at the speakers' table. Other organizations are in a position that makes it necessary to seat a good many people in places of honor, occasionally so many that a single table is not adequate, and a two-tiered or even a three-tiered head table is required.

In the case of a two-tiered table, it is optional whether the lower or the upper one is the place of greater importance, and it depends upon the judgment of the chairman as to which is chosen as the primary table. If the head table is three-tiered, the middle one is the most important.

In this age of enlightenment it may seem strange that the question of whether or not to seat thirteen at a table ever arises. It does, though, and a thoughtful host or hostess will not discount the fact that some of the old superstitions die hard and that at least one guest may feel squeamish about being one of thirteen. This point of view is not shared by all, and from time to time one finds a chairman who deliberately flouts the ancient fear and purposely surrounds himself with twelve others.

Having determined the number of guests to be at the head table, the next step is to make a list of those whom you will invite. Start with the ones who definitely must be there: the president; perhaps other officers and the program chairman; the speaker and his wife (or her husband) if the spouse has come along; minister, priest, or rabbi, if an invocation and benediction are to be given; others who are to have any part in the program; then those in the community who for good reason should be honored with an invitation.

Examples of the last mentioned might be: the mayor of the city; local people who are outstanding representatives of the interests of the speaker (e.g., if he is presenting a medical subject, the president of the local Academy of Medicine); newspaper editors; heads of leading educational and cultural institutions; representatives of social agencies; those known as civic leaders.

Reference was made earlier to invocation and benediction. The decision as to whether or not to include these in the agenda must be made by the organization presenting the program. Often they are automatically included by virtue of constitution and by-laws, and in this case a member sometimes assumes this duty. However, for a large meeting, especially one of a civic nature, it is quite usual to have both invocation and benediction. In large communities where there is a cosmopolitan population including representatives of the three major faiths it is customary to have a clergyman of either of the two Christian faiths give either invocation or benediction, and a Jewish rabbi give the other.

Having composed the guest list, the next step is to issue invitations. Before doing this, arrange with the place where your meeting is to be held, for a spot where head table guests may foregather and then proceed to the dining room. It may be a separate room or, if this is not available, some sheltered corner near the door through which entrance will be made.

There are two ways of issuing an invitation: by telephone or by letter. The first is informal and has the advantage of saving the invitee the trouble of returning a mailed acceptance. However, even if a telephoned acceptance is received, it should be followed by a brief note of confirmation giving details of date, time, and place of foregathering. If a written invitation is sent, it may include the information about the gathering place, thus saving a second communication. The written invitation may also provide a telephone number to which acceptance or rejection may be called, indicating that a written response is not necessary or expected. In this age of over-business such a timesaver is welcome.

Here is a fine example of an invitation to be seated at the head table:

"Miss —— ——
325 Superior Avenue
Cleveland, Ohio 44114

Dear Miss ——:
        The Nationalities Services Center of Cleveland will present its first annual Golden Door Award to Maestro George Szell of the Cleveland Symphony Orchestra, on Saturday September 17, 1966, at a civic luncheon to be held in the Grand Ballroom of the Statler-Hilton Hotel.
        The Golden Door Award was established by the American Council for Nationalities Service several years ago, to honor Americans of foreign birth who have made distinguished contributions to American life and culture. As an active member of both the American Council and the Cleveland Welfare Federation, the Center takes great pride in having the opportunity to recognize Maestro Szell's great contributions to Cleveland and to our Nation.
        As a co-chairman of the award luncheon, I write to ask you to give us the great honor of sitting with us at our Speaker's Table. I am certain that you are well aware of the need we feel to make this civic luncheon the success it should be, and of the obvious need we have, therefore, of your participation with us. We shall assemble at noon that day in the Ohio Room and proceed from there to the platform sharply at 12:30.
        For your convenience I enclose a return addressed reply card concerning our request, and am most hopeful that we may count on your being with us that day.
        Thanking you in advance for your helpfulness, I am,
                            Sincerely,

                    (signed) Kenyon C. Bolton"

The following is a copy of the stamped and addressed reply card mentioned in the letter:

"—— I accept your Nationalities Services Center Civic Luncheon invitation to join you at noon in the Ohio Room of the Statler-Hilton Hotel, on Saturday, September 17th, and from there proceed to the Ballroom and sit at the Speaker's Table.

—— I regret my inability to be with you for the Nationalities Services Center Civic Luncheon on Saturday, September 17th.

(signed) .... "

This invitation* is included not merely as an example of
form and wording, but because it is a perfect and actual
illustration of the kind of civic occasion described in Chapter
Two.

Ideally the invitation to be seated at the head table
should go out four weeks before the event, unlike the general
invitation for which two weeks is ordinarily adequate. The
reason for this is obvious: prospective guests are likely to
have full calendars, and sufficient time must be allowed for
replacing those who send their regrets.

Even though you have firm acceptances from your guests
it is still a good idea to give them a telephoned reminder a
day or two before the meeting.

Now that you know who your guests are going to be, the
next step is to plan their seating. A very simple chart may
be drawn to make this easier:**

Of course as many sections are drawn as there will be
guests. Some organizations that have very frequent meal
functions have this type of chart either printed or mimeographed.

In planning your seating, place the presiding officer to
the right (audience's left) of the lectern. The most important
guest, usually the speaker, or the most eminent of the speak-

---

* Mr. Bolton gave his permission to use the letter and card verbatim.
** See Appendix for other suggested charts.

ers if you have more than one—is seated to the presiding officer's right. If the mayor attends, however, he should have that place of honor at the chairman's right. In placing the person at the left of the lectern, remember that he will have no one on his right with whom he can converse, or at least there will be an awkward space between him and the chairman. An officer of the organization is usually given this place in order to avoid putting an outside guest in an uncomfortable position.

Not all speakers' tables have the lectern either permanently set, or in place while the meal is being served, so that this point does not always need to be taken into consideration. In some dining areas, possibly most of them, a portable lectern is brought in when the speaking starts.

Bearing in mind the thought that the immediate right of the chairman is the most honored position, and if there is no lectern as a barrier to conversation, his immediate left the next most honored, arrange your guests' seating at your discretion keeping those who are to participate close to the center. If there is a lectern with an officer to its left, the second most honored position would be to the left of that officer. Ordinarily there are fewer women than men at head tables, unless it is exclusively a women's organization, and they should be spaced appropriately. Although there is no rule that says a woman should not be seated at the very ends of the speakers' table, it is discourteous to do so, and does not look well from the audience. Of course, when the majority of the guests are women, seating at the ends can not be avoided.

Rare situations arise when it is necessary to observe the strictest protocol in seating a head table. If high government officials or representatives of foreign governments are being presented, this would certainly be true. Consular representatives may be among the guests in the latter case, and it is necessary to know which country's representatives take precedence over others'. An inquiry made in advance of the event can avoid hurt feelings and even lasting antagonisms. In the case of our high government officials, usually a special secretary or other agent is assigned to help the local person with correct seating. There are still places below and above the salt!

When your guest list is complete and your chart made, you are ready to think of place cards. The kind you select will depend upon the formality of the occasion, but plain white is never wrong. For very formal occasions the names should be professionally hand-lettered, but for less formal events they may be written (never typewritten) or printed legibly by hand. Last names only with the appropriate title (Mr., Mrs., Miss, Dr., etc.) should be used. It will be simple to place these cards on the table when the time comes, using the chart you have already made.

Reference has been made to the importance of decorations, and this point can not be overemphasized. A maitre d'hotel, or his equivalent in another location, usually takes pride in what he has available to make his tables, and especially the head table, look well. If you have a color scheme, let him know what it is and take his suggestions. If your meeting is a very large one and you are consequently assembling in a huge room, be sure that your decorations at the head table are large and colorful enough to be plainly visible. In these times of handsome artificial floral arrangements, many hotels have a varied supply of these which may be used effectively in lieu of natural blooms. If fresh flowers are used, you are responsible for ordering them and of course for paying for them. It is always important *to know what you want* and to be articulate about it to those with whom you are working. They want to be helpful, but they also need to be helped to be so.

One important matter which is easily overlooked and which should be arranged ahead of time is the point at which tables should be cleared. Sometimes the management wants all clearing done before the program starts. Usually, however, consent will be given to leave dessert plates and coffee cups until after adjournment. But whichever arrangement is made, the chairman should know what to expect. The experienced chairman also spots the head waiter before the meeting and arranges with him for a signal when the tables are cleared and the proceedings may start.

There are two remaining preliminary steps to be made: prepare the introductions for the speakers' table and organize the agenda. The former task would be accomplished by the one who has had charge of arranging the head table; the latter would be strictly the responsibility of the presiding officer.

The agenda might look something like this:

Blankville College Club
Annual Meeting
May 25, 19 - -, 12 Noon

Agenda

   I. 12 Noon, Invocation. (Present the Rev. William Smith)
  II. 12:15—1:00 P.M. Eat Lunch
 III. 1:00—1:15 P.M. Introduce speakers' table. (Use attached list)*
  IV. 1:15—1:45 P.M. Address by ———. (Introduction of speaker on attached sheet)*
   V. 1:45 P.M. Thank speaker and introduce Mme. ———
  VI. 1:48 P.M. Solo, TAKE JOY HOME, sung by Mme. ———
 VII. 1:55 P.M. Thank Mme. ——— and present Rabbi Robert Levy, who will give the Benediction
VIII. Adjournment

It may seem that this agenda is given in unnecessary detail, but everyone who has presided at a large affair knows how easy it is to have the mind go blank at a crucial moment.

With all the preparations made, the day of the meeting arrives. Let us suppose that it is a very large function. Chairman, program chairman and person in charge of the speakers' table have arrived early and have gathered in the appointed meeting room to wait for guests. To facilitate arranging the lineup for entry into the dining room the chairman has asked that chairs corresponding to the number of guests be placed in this waiting room and ranged along the wall. Slips of paper with names of the guests plainly

---

* See Appendix for sample introductions of speakers and speakers' table.

marked on them are placed on these chairs,* perhaps fastened down with scotch tape, in the order in which the guests are to proceed to the dining room and take their places at the head table. This done, one of the welcoming group stations himself at a place close to where guests will be arriving—elevator or doorway—and is ready to usher them into the gathering place.

Sometimes the dining room is situated at considerable distance from the place where guests have assembled. In any event, it is a good idea to have someone assigned to lining up the head table guests and escorting them right to the table. Often there is at least one step to negotiate to reach the platform, and the escort may complete his duties by helping the guests maneuvre that potential hazard.

The people at the head table have been arbitrarily referred to as guests. They are not always that in the literal sense of the word, for occasionally an organization whose budget is at low ebb expects even those seated in the places of honor to pay for their tickets and only the speakers are guests in the true sense of the word.

With all the preliminaries accomplished, everyone settles down to enjoy the meal. The possible exception to this may be the presiding officer who still has a long agenda to cover before adjournment is called for.

Very likely one of the most trying tasks which faces the chairman is the introduction of the speakers' table, especially if it is a long one, includes many people who are not personally known to him, and if there have been last-minute changes in the list, as there all too frequently are.

However, as has been indicated, the chairman should either make or be provided with a list of those at the head table, arranged according to their position at the table, with a few *brief* introductory notes about each. But even though introductions are brief, be sure that they are absolutely ac-

---

* This device of placing names on chairs has been used very successfully and has often been a conversational ice-breaker. I do not know how generally it is employed, but I highly recommend it.

curate. It is always an affront to present anyone incorrectly, and doubly so when it is done publicly. The chairman has decided ahead of time what procedure he will follow in making the introductions, and will start at his right, the audience's left, and proceed straight across the table, only mentioning the names of those who are to speak and indicating that they will be introduced later. Introductions are always made beginning at the right, but the chairman has one alternative* in procedure: he may introduce all those on his right (except speakers, of course) and then start at his far left and present all those at that side of the table. In the case of a multi-tiered head table, the guests at the primary table should be introduced last, and if it is three-tiered, choice of which of the other two to introduce first is optional. In making the introductions of all the tables, do so from right to left.

These are the only ways of making the introductions, unless the occasion is a very informal one and the chairman and the audience well known to each other.

The matter of applause following introductions has been handled in a variety of ways. Some chairmen let it ring forth unrestrained after each presentation. Others feel that too much time is consumed in this way and ask that all applause be held until all guests have been introduced. At least one chairman** follows a procedure which he himself invented: he allows just one clap for each person introduced. To achieve complete efficiency in this area some organizations print a list of those at the head table either on a separate sheet of paper or on the back of the program which contains not only the agenda but also the menu offered. This again is done for more formal affairs.

The chairman now has only one major task remaining: to introduce the speaker—or speakers—of the day. All introductory information should have been received long ago*** and the chairman should have everything to be said

---

* See sample in Appendix.
** Curtis Lee Smith, President of the Cleveland Chamber of Commerce.
*** See Chapter Four.

either committed to memory or in readable form in his hands, and available without fumbling and rattling papers. An introduction should be brief and to the point, bearing in mind that the audience is there not to hear the introducer but the speaker. On the other hand, it should not be as brief as this introduction which was actually made by one chairman: "I have been asked to introduce Dr. ———, who will speak to you on DICKENS AND HIS CENTURY. I have now done so. He will now do so." There is a golden mean in introductions as in everything.

There is nothing to be done now except to listen to the rest of the program, give gracious thanks to all who have contributed to the success of the meeting, and then adjourn it.

10

THE CHAIRMAN

The person who presides at any meeting, large or small, is like the star in a drama. The success of the meeting literally depends upon him, or her, just as the success of a play hinges upon the performance of its star. Indeed, those who have frequent occasion to conduct meetings in public would do well to take a leaf or two from the books of successful actors. Anyone who has been exposed to years of either observing or participating in meetings has formed the habit of watching all public performers, whether professional or amateur, learning much from what he sees and hears.

If you have been elected to serve as chairman of an organization, or appointed to preside over one special affair, it may be taken for granted that this has happened because you are obviously capable of fulfilling this type of responsibility creditably. This is nearly always the case, although there have been notable exceptions to the rule, when appointments have been made through a sense of obligation, because of social position, or because of inner quid-pro-quo politics.

But no matter how a person comes to his responsibility as presiding officer, it is really up to him to take stock of himself and make sure that he measures up. Socrates' command, "Know thyself," is always applicable and especially so in the cases of those in positions of command. Where limitations are recognized, they can be remedied.

A chairman should first of all understand that the position is going to demand time and work, and if he is not willing to accept this basic fact, he should not accept the honor. This applies whether it is the continuing presidency of an organization or the one-time chairmanship of a function. These, of course, are two very different things, and the former carries far the graver responsibility.

Briefly, the presidency involves all the duties of an executive: planning, organizing, making sure that plans are carried out by those to whom they are delegated. In previous chapters whenever a special committee was mentioned, emphasis was always placed on the need for the head of the organization to work with that committee, to be carefully informed on all its activities, to counsel and give direction when necessary. Like all good executives, however, the organization chairman too should allow his committee chairmen and members sufficient freedom to develop plans and carry them out without making his authority suffocatingly felt. It is said that women chairmen are most often guilty of "authoritarianism," least willing to relinquish an iota of what they consider the prerogatives of their office. If this seems true, it is probably because there are many more women's organizations than there are men's, and consequently more women chairmen. Also, women are inclined to take their office-holding more seriously since frequently it is their main interest, whereas with men it is a hobby, a side issue, with their work careers holding the center of interest in their lives.

Any person who conducts meetings, whether frequently or seldom, should know enough about parliamentary procedure* to allow him to function according to the rules of the game. Only rarely does he have to put every slightest direction into practice, but just as one would not venture out into society without knowing the fundamentals of etiquette, just so no one should undertake to conduct a meeting without some knowledge of parliamentary rules of order.

At the same time it is not necessary to become a slave to the rules, and certainly there are times when they may be relaxed. Nothing is more irksome than the chairman of a

---

* John Q. Tilson. *A Manual of Parliamentary Procedure.* N. Y. Oceana Publishing Co. 1949.

small informal committee who holds literally to every rule in the book, when the committee is deciding such a momentous matter as whether to have chicken-a-la-king or fruit salad for its next monthly meeting. A good chairman knows that there are times for strict adherence to rules and times when they can be set to one side.

For very formal occasions when it is necessary to adhere strictly to the letter of the law, large organizations employ a parliamentarian in order to insure that no errors are made in the conduct of the meeting.

The need for careful preparation of any type of meeting has already been stressed, and it is one of the chairman's duties to be sure that such preparations have been made and faithfully carried out. Even though others have been doing the actual work, the results should be firmly held in the chairman's own hands, so that he or she comes to the meeting serenely confident that everything humanly possible has been done to insure the success of the meeting over which he is to preside.

As the meeting opens it is important to communicate this sense of quiet confidence to those present. People are quick to sense absence of confidence or nervousness, and this can spoil their total enjoyment of an occasion. The chairman should think of himself as a host, and just as a host in his own home considers the comfort of his guests above all else, so the chairman should think of the comfort of those in the audience before him.

Physical details of arrangements have been attended to beforehand and presumably everyone is comfortably seated, whether at tables or in rows. If people are standing and you, from the vantage point of being at the front of the room and conceivably standing on a dais, see empty chairs, it is perfectly proper to indicate the empty places and allow time for the standees to be seated.

Be sure that your voice can be plainly heard throughout the room. The microphones have been tested, but don't depend too much on their effectiveness. Ask if everyone in the room can hear you, and later be equally watchful and

solicitous that they hear others on the program. Often someone is stationed at the rear of the room to signal the chairman if the voices are not carrying to the back.

It goes without saying that you have started the meeting
on time. It is always a great temptation to put off the
opening moment. You see people still coming in at the door,
still looking around for seats, or if it is a meal function you
notice that some are still eating desserts—but in spite of
everything, resist the temptation and *start on time.* There
will always be latecomers. Some even come straggling in
when the meeting is practically over. If people are still eating when you start, do refrain from making that well-worn
and feeble effort at humor: "If those who are still eating
will please do so quietly. . . ."

This next suggestion may seem either superfluous or
silly, but it is given in good faith as an important point to
keep in mind. Smile when you open the meeting and greet
your guests. Even though you are nervous, smile and let
your pleasure at being there show. All of us have seen
presiding officers at any kind of meeting look so harassed
and anxious that some of that feeling is communicated to
the audience, sometimes to such a degree that their attention
falters.

Don't ever start your meeting with an apology—for
weather (which isn't your fault), for poor attendance, for
the fact that you are competing with other attractions, or
for anything else. If the weather is especially bad, a word of
commendation for those who braved the elements might be
in order. Have you ever been at a meeting where the chairman roundly scolded those who were there, because the crowd
was so small? Nothing could be more illogical, for those who
were not there deserved the scolding. The chairman should
be tactful and never say or do anything that might offend
anyone present. This means having very sensitive antennae
constantly extended.

Keep your meeting moving. You should have a time
schedule, as indicated in the preceding chapter, and even
if that can not be followed down to the split second, follow

it to within two seconds. Earlier the meeting chairman was compared to the star of a dramatic performance, and the comparison holds good here too, for proper timing is an important ingredient of dramatic genius. No one who attends meetings has escaped the one that drags on for many minutes longer than its schedule has called for. Usually this is the fault of the chairman whose announcements have been too lengthy or whose introductions have been too flowery and involved. If you have ever been the speaker at such a meeting you know what agony you live through waiting for these preliminaries to be completed while your audience one by one tiptoes out of the room either through sheer boredom or to keep appointments that can not wait.

If you have guest speakers, leave the business part of your meeting until after they have spoken, so that they may have the privilege of leaving if they wish. Especially if you have free speakers who have been told that your funds do not allow you to pay a fee, do not give a detailed financial report which reveals that you have several thousand dollars in the bank. This has been known to happen.

Actually, if possible, eliminate all business reports on days when you have guest speakers, if your constitution permits it. Your meeting should end on a high note, and if you follow a good program with dull reports a rapid descent is made from keen interest to tedium.

It would hardly seem necessary to admonish a chairman to stay in the meeting after he has made the introductions, but there are some who do not observe this basic courtesy. They slip from the platform and use the time of the speaker's talk to smoke in the hall, buttonhole fellow members, or just lounge. This happens routinely at political conventions and even at local political meetings, as anyone knows to his sorrow if he has ever had to make any kind of presentation to them. It shouldn't happen at any kind of meeting.

It is for the chairman to decide the order of speakers if a number of them are scheduled to appear on the same program. Usually the best one—or at least the best-known one—is presented last. The second-best usually speaks first, and the least-known or least competent, in the middle. Seldom are there more than three on a program. It has happened that the one placed in the middle spot turns out to be a sleeper and surprises everyone by being the best of the lot.

It has been said before, but it bears repeating: no matter how many speakers you have on your program, be sure that each one knows how much time he is allowed. Then hold him to that by giving him signals which have been prearranged. Remember that one of your main duties is to keep the meeting moving.

As chairman you have the responsibility of introducing your performers. If they have given you material in advance, as they have been asked to do, use it. If they have not replied to your request for biographical information, do some research in the various WHO'S WHOs that are available. If they are not listed in any of them, ask for some data before the meeting and jot down whatever pertinent facts you can obtain in a short time. Unless you know the speaker very well, and unless the audience knows him well, never try to tell stories at his expense.

If your meeting has been a failure—or if you feel as if it has (the two are not always the same), don't let your feelings be seen. If your speaker proves a disappointment, treat him as graciously as if he had been a great success, and don't apologize, even obliquely, to the audience. It is a temptation to do this, especially if you are convinced that a speaker has given false or incorrect information. The only thing you can do is to make a mental note never to invite him to speak again, and to plan a program for the very near future which will correct the misinformation which he has given.

Never ask for questions following a program unless you really want them and unless there is sufficient time left. If there are questions, repeat each one clearly so that the audience does not have the frustrating experience of hearing only the answers. Also, protect your speaker from obviously crackpot questioners by tactfully eliminating such questions as they are asked.

Some talks, especially the inspirational ones, simply do not lend themselves to questions, and their whole effect is lost if an attempt is made to conduct a question period after such a program.

As has been said, a good meeting should end on a high note, and it is the chairman who must see that this happens. Sometimes a program is so good that you will not want to say a word after it, except thank you, for fear of spoiling it.

But if your speaker has let you down, you can still bring the end of the meeting back to a higher plane by your own final remarks—tactful thanks to the speaker, possibly comments on what the talk has meant to you, and announcements about future meeting. Some chairmen plan a routine, almost ritualistic, closing to all their meetings, with a verse or a song which everyone joins in singing. But this kind of thing can be done only when the same group attends all the organization's programs.

When all is said and done, much depends upon the ingenuity and the native tact of the presiding officer, and more so at the close of the meeting than at any other point. Everything may be foreseen and planned for, except the effect of the speaker upon his audience and the atmosphere which will be generated by what he has said. It is the ending of a program which really tests the chairman's mettle.

11

YOUR GUESTS

From observing a good many meetings it would seem that the last item for consideration is the guests, not so much those who are regular members of an organization as those who may be attracted to an open meeting because they were interested in the subject or the speaker, or simply because they wanted to come to be with other people for a little while.

A great deal of time and thought is spent on attracting people to a meeting, but not nearly so much is given to how they should be treated after they get there.

Until the actual day of the event, a guest is only a name, and possibly only a number. He has been sent a ticket, if tickets are being used, or informed that his ticket will be waiting for him at the door. If no advance reservations are required, even less is known of the prospective guest. He is neither a name nor a number, but only a potential presence.

The Hospitality Committee is the one responsible for the treatment of guests, and it is one of those designated as a standing committee, although again a special one may be appointed for a particular occasion. The Hospitality Committee should be thought of as one of the most important in creating the public image of an organization.

We have listed the desirable characteristics of the chairmen of other types of committees in some detail. For the chairman—and the members—of the Hospitality Committee it is really necessary to say only that they should be deeply and genuinely interested in helping people feel at their ease and in placing them where they will be happiest and enjoy themselves the most.

Affairs that are planned by women are likely to be more considerate of their guests than those planned by men, probably because women are accustomed to assuming the main responsibility for hospitality in their own homes. There may be another reason for this, too. Women have not developed the hail-fellow-well-met approach that men have with one another, and they are more inclined to wait for overtures to be made by others, especially if they are new to a group, and to have more understanding of the necessity sometimes to go more than half way in making people feel at home.

Certain techniques have been tried in efforts to help guests feel at ease. In a small group this is not too difficult, for in such groups every member can act as a welcomer. Indeed this happens almost spontaneously, for in any established group there is a high degree of natural curiosity about new people. There is no anonymity in the smaller group, and those who join are not seeking it.

It is in the large, impersonal affairs that ways of helping the guest to feel comfortable need to be employed. Those who make the first contact are often ticket-takers or ticket-sellers, and these people become so busy if a large crowd is involved that they hardly have the opportunity to look at the person who stands before them, let alone take time to be gracious.

At most large meal functions a corps of hostesses (sometimes hosts are included) is put in charge of meeting the guests as they come through the door, directing them to the checking area if this is necessary, answering questions, and helping them to find their places. If table assignments are noted on the tickets, this is comparatively easy. If there are no reserved places, the hostesses keep one another informed by a system of signals where the vacant places are. Hosts or hostesses should wear easily seen badges, so that they may be readily identified.

In this connection the need for briefing those who have this particular responsibility must be stressed. Nothing can create an air of utter confusion more rapidly than a group of hostesses who do not know what they are supposed to be doing. A briefing session may be scheduled on the day of the meeting itself, at an hour well in advance of the opening time. However, it is better to hold it a day or two before, so that no pressure is felt when the very early guests begin to arrive—as they do—at least half an hour ahead of time. The chairman of the Hospitality Committee is the logical person to do the briefing, and she should be prepared to assign a definite post to each hostess, and to designate the area of the room for which each should be responsible. Ideally each hostess should be given a chart* showing the location of all chairs and tables in the room. Suggestions should be given about attitude and conduct: the former should be eager helpfulness, the latter brisk courtesy. Probably you too have been present at affairs where the hostesses acted as though they hated everyone and wished that they were anywhere but there. If you are going to have a system of signalling the location of empty places, this should be worked out during the briefing period.

The guest who arrives too early sometimes presents a problem which may be solved simply by not opening the doors until a certain set time. Here the hostesses have the task of courteously explaining to the early birds that they must wait for the doors to open. This measure is often a practical necessity, for many times waiters are setting the tables until the last minute.

If you are coping with a very large affair and feel inadequate to train your hostesses, you might turn for help to a local restaurant whose hostesses are known for their graciousness and efficiency. The management of such restaurants has been known to send their head hostess out to help with training amateurs, realizing that such a gesture has great public relations value.

During the briefing period, the hostesses should be instructed about what to do when confronted by irate guests.

---

* See sample in Appendix.

These are almost inevitable at a large function, especially if seating is by assignment and not by choice. The individual hostess should not be expected to cope with such situations all by herself, for a number of obvious reasons. Either the chairman of the Hospitality Committee or of the Arrangements Committee should be easily accessible to deal with the complainers. If all this is prearranged, the chances for unpleasant confusion are considerably lessened.

Some organizations which regularly present large meal functions have adopted the device of assigning a hostess—or host—to each table. These persons have been given the very definite task of presiding at that table much as they would at the dining table in their own homes. That is, guests are introduced to one another and an effort is made to keep rolling a ball of conversation which involves everyone at the table.

For sophisticated meeting-goers—and there are many of these—none of this will be necessary. This breed, which has always been with us but which has multiplied in the last twenty years, does not attend meetings aimlessly but for very good educational, social, and cultural reasons. They are very likely to sweep past hostesses, know exactly where they want to sit, and as soon as others appear at the table introduce themselves. They are always welcome, for almost without knowing they are doing it, they make of the meeting a much more enjoyable occasion for those who happen to be at their tables.

It is not of these that the Hospitality Committee needs to think when it is laying its plans, but rather of the shy and retiring person who ventures out only once or twice a year and for whom the price of a luncheon or dinner ticket represents a sacrificial expenditure. We should use every bit of ingenuity we possess to make this person comfortable and make the whole occasion memorable for her, or him—but usually her.

Not all functions involve sitting down at a table, although these are the ones which come first to mind when hospitality is considered. In the formal, auditorium style of meeting there is no real need for putting people at their ease in the same way that we do when they break bread together. In this situation efficient ushers can do all that is required. These too should be briefed concerning their duties, which are simple: first, to help people get seated, and second, to distribute programs and other materials if this is called for. The usher, like the hostess, should be pleasant and eager to help. The greatest challenges to ushers, as everyone knows, is to get the audience to sit up close to the front, and to move in to the centers of the rows. It often seems as if everyone's favorite seat is the very end one of the very last row.

There is a third type of function: the standing-up tea or cocktail party, usually held to honor the speaker—and here too the Hospitality Committee needs to be on the qui vive, not so much for the latter as for the former. There is something about a cocktail party which generates its own informality, and it is rare to see lone people at these affairs standing in corners forlornly wishing that they had never come. Good members of a hospitality committee keep their eyes open for just such guests and immediately approach them to draw them into a group. Often this person is a newcomer to town, who has not yet had the opportunity to make friends and who is eager to do so. Anyone who has ever been in this situation himself knows how grateful one can be to the thoughtful host or hostess who has seen his plight and has come to the rescue. This should not be left to chance as it too frequently is, but certain members of the organization should be given the definite assignment of taking care of the obviously neglected and solitary guests.

In considering all the responsibilities that others have towards the guests, we should not lose sight of the fact that guests too have some duties, and that those who present meetings have the right to expect them to fulfill these:

Guests should come on time, and if they are tardy for a good reason, should seat themselves as unobstrusively as possible. Sometimes the back rows are reserved for latecomers, and if this is the case, the tardy guest should seat himself there without protest, and not sneak up front the minute the lights are out or the hostess's back is turned.

Those who come on time should willingly and cheerfully sit in front, and move to the center of the row, instead of blocking the way for those who arrive later.

A guest should not complain about conditions which can not be remedied. The pillar behind which he is seated can not be removed before the meeting starts. If he came late, the only seats left are the less desirable ones.

No matter what kind of meeting it is, a guest should be courteously attentive. Even if the program is a disappointing bore, he should still observe the amenities, even if it has to be feigned.

From the point of view of the speaker and other members of the audience nothing is more annoying than the whisperers, those who carry on a running sotto voce conversation with companions throughout a program. The chairman has every right quietly and unobstrusively to reprimand these people. Some organizations delegate this duty to ushers, who need to be especially watchful if a program takes place with lights out.

The guest who comes to a meeting armed with rustling paper bags presents another annoyance for those around him. Again, some groups insist that such impediments be checked in advance, or placed in a designated spot at the rear of the room.

The guests who can not sit through a meeting without nibbling chocolate or sucking cough drops can be another source of annoyance to a chairman, especially if the refreshments are wrapped in cellophane which can sound like an atomic explosion if worked on in a quiet room. But unless the meeting is held in a public place where eating is forbidden, there is not much a chairman can do about this. This problem is likely to arise only in meetings open to a wide public.

Guests and members should approach every meeting, regular or special, with the feeling that they are coming to something gala, like the pleasant anticipation of opening a surprise gift.

A really memorable meeting results only when officers, members and guests all function actively in their respective roles. This happens seldom enough, but when it does, no one ever forgets it.

12

WAS IT A GOOD MEETING?

Before we answer that question, we have to ask another: what is a good meeting?

We can list certain tangible requirements and make sure that they were all provided and executed correctly. These have been indicated throughout the preceding chapters, but in summary the following would be the retrospective check-list by which you as chairman might give your meeting one kind of evaluation:

> Was the room in which it was held large enough, light enough, well-ventilated, quiet?
> Were the chairs comfortable and efficiently arranged?
> Did the microphone work properly?
> Did your audience come up to your expectations, both quantitatively and qualitatively?
> Were all the needs of your speakers or other performers anticipated, or was there last-minute confusion?
> Did your hosts, hostesses or ushers function as they were expected to, and was seating accomplished smoothly and quickly?
> Were the meal and service satisfactory?
> Did you keep the meeting moving, or did it drag?

You may answer all these questions favorably and still come away with the uneasy feeling that something wasn't right.

The sense that a meeting was good or bad can come to you without benefit of evaluation sheets, although these are helpful up to a point. But there are imponderables over and above the specifics of arrangements and careful advance planning which leave nothing to chance.

A good meeting is impossible of attainment without all these specifics, but there are other ingredients which push a meeting beyond the category of the good and into the rare class of the *excellent*.

The stunning impact of a speaker upon his audience, the electric spark of attentiveness and involvement which you can almost see and hear in an audience, the alert, interested poise of heads and eyes, the sense that *you* on the platform and *they* in the audience are working together to create an hour which none of you will forget, and which may even change the course of some lives—all this can happen, and if it does only once in a lifetime, it can make all meetings seem worth all the trouble it may take to prepare and present them.

All this could happen oftener, if we applied to our planning and execution of meetings every single thing we know which would help them to achieve greater meaningfulness.

Meetings are a great instrument of our time and our culture, and they should be given every thoughtful care of which we are capable.

APPENDICES

APPENDIX I

SELECTED READINGS

Stuart Chase, in collaboration with Marian Chase. *Roads to Agreement*. New York: Harper & Bros., 1951. 240 pp. (o.p.)*
Tells about different ways in which groups have worked successfully. Main interest is in the small discussion group rather than in the large meeting.

Elizabeth Downs. *Let's Make Plans* (a guide for clubwomen). New York: Alfred Knopf, 1942. 246 pp. (o.p.)
Just what it says it is, this book gives practical advice to clubwomen. Some of it is outdated, but basically it is sound.

Hal Golden and Kitty Hanson. *How to Plan, Produce and Publicize Special Events*. New York: Oceana Publications, Inc., 1960. 256 pp.
A detailed and practical manual which will be of special help to those planning large functions.

Edward J. Hegarty. *How to Run Better Meetings*. New York: McGraw-Hill, 1957. 312 pp.
This would prove especially helpful to men planning meetings of every kind. It is written from their point of view and directed at them.

A. Liebers. *How to Organize a Club*. Dobbs Ferry, N. Y.: Oceana Publications, Inc., 1953. 64 pp.

Lucy R. Milligan and Harold V. Milligan. *The Club Member's Handbook*. New York: Barnes and Noble, Inc., 1942. 300 pp. (o.p.)
One of the most practical in its field.

---

* (o.p.) out of print.

Harry Simons. *How to Run a Club.* New York: Harper & Bros., 1955. 308 pp. (o.p.)
>Again, practical advice on organization and conduct of regular meetings.

Frank Snell. *How to Hold a Better Meeting.* New York: Harper & Bros., 1958. 148 pp. (o. p.)
>This book is entirely devoted to the kind of meeting held by business and industry, concentrating on problem solving and decision making. Very specialized and good in its field.

Herbert A. Thelen. *Dynamics of Groups at Work.* Chicago: The University of Chicago Press, 1954. 379 pp.
>A very scholarly work on group dynamics. The chapter on *Effective Meetings* (p. 181 ff) is an analysis of what really goes on in a meeting, action and interaction between people.

John Q. Tilson. *How to Conduct a Meeting.* New York: Oceana Publications, Inc., 1950. 64 pp.
>In pamphlet form, this gives practical directions on the subject stated in its title.

————. *A Manual of Parliamentary Procedure.* New York: Oceana Publications, Inc., 1949. 149 pp.
>Parliamentary rules from A to Z in simple and understandable form.

MAGAZINES

Adult Leadership, a journal issued monthly by the Adult Education Association of the U.S.A., 743 N. Wabash Avenue, Chicago, Illinois

Program, Published bi-monthly from September to June by Platform Publishing Co., 54 West 40th St., New York, N. Y.
>The first of these journals has frequent articles about the group process. The second is a mine of practical information for the program planner.

APPENDIX II

Examples of Two Program Planning Institutes which actually took place and met with success.

The first of these was held on two days, a week apart. It

was sponsored by an Adult Education Council. The second one took place all in one day and was presented by a large public library.

EXAMPLE I

INSTITUTE FOR PROGRAM PLANNERS AND
CLUB LEADERS
June 3, 19. .

10:15 A.M.

I. Why Are We Getting Together?
(This was an explanation, made by three people, of why it was believed that this Institute would benefit the community.)

II. Making Meetings Click
(Those in the audience listed their programming problems and turned them in to the chairman for later consideration.)

12:00 Noon
Time out for lunch.

1:45 P.M.

III. Making Meetings Click (continued)
(A panel of experts analyzed the program problems which the audience had submitted at the morning session.)

June 10, 19. .
10:45 A.M.

I. How to Read Two Books
(This was a discussion of reading with a purpose and how it might benefit the program planner.)

II. How to Hold an Audience
(Pointers on presenting programs.)

III. Methods of Getting Along with People
(How to get the group to work more closely together.)

12:00 Noon
Time out for lunch.

1:45 P.M.

I. Demonstrations of Sample Programs

   A. Using books and musical recordings.
      (Mrs. H...... S...... gave highlights from the life
      of Franz Schubert, and played some recordings of his
      music.)
   B. A film followed by discussion.
      (Mrs. W...... W. M...... led a discussion of the
      film "Does It Matter What You Think?")
   C. Book review followed by discussion.
      (James B. Conant's *Slums and Suburbs* was reviewed
      by Dr. M...... S.......)

EXAMPLE II

THIRD ANNUAL PROGRAM PLANNING CONFERENCE
Friday, June 28, 19..
Morning Session—9:45 A.M. - 12:00 M.

Welcome (This was given by the assistant director of the library
presenting the Institute.)
Keynote Address: Club Women and Community Service
(By the Editor of one of the daily newspapers.)
The Program Committee Meets. (A meeting was role-played on
the platform.)
Using Films on Your Club Program.
Publicity Panel. (Here representatives of three newspapers and
two radio stations told how to get effective publicity.)

Luncheon, 12 Noon - 1:15 P.M.—in the Library cafeteria.
Afternoon Session—1:30 P.M. - 3:30 P.M.

Community Resources for Program Planners. (This was a symposium with five members presenting resources for the
following topics:
        Civic and Local Government
        National and International Affairs
        Community Welfare
        Family Health and Welfare
        Cultural and Educational)

Note that the hours for the sessions were set at times which would be most convenient for the women attending. The same types of programs have been presented during the evening so that men might attend.

APPENDIX III

LIST OF SOME LECTURE BUREAUS*

Adult Education Council of Greater Chicago
332 South Michigan Avenue, Chicago, Illinois 60604
Tel. (312) 427-2670

American Program Bureau
2 Park Square, Boston, Massachusetts 02116
Tel. (617) LIberty 2-6353-4

Ricklie Boasberg-Hoyt Bureau
2653 North Moreland Boulevard, Cleveland, Ohio 44120
Tel. (216) 991-4811

The Giesen Management, Inc.
111 West 57 Street, New York, N. Y. 10019
Tel. (212) COlumbus 5-0862

W. Colston Leigh, Inc.
521 Fifth Avenue, New York, N. Y. 10017
Tel. (212) MUrray Hill 2-6623

77 West Washington Street, Chicago, Illinois 60602
Tel. (312) CEntral 6-3541
Russ Building, San Francisco, California 94104
Tel. (415) EXbrook 2-7147

Ann Lewis Program Service
97 Port Washington Boulevard, Roslyn, N. Y. 11526
Tel. (516) MAin 7-0054 & 4772

Marsh Program Service
P. O. Box 203, Newtonville, Massachusetts 02160
Tel. (617) BIgelow 4-6544

---

* All are listed with the permission of the Bureaus. Listing is for information and does not necessarily constitute a recommendation.

National Lecture Bureau
  General offices,
  104 South Michigan Avenue, Chicago, Illinois 60603
    Tel. (312) 782-2257

The Redpath Bureau
  343 South Dearborn Street, Chicago, Illinois 60604
    Tel. (312) HArrison 7-8723

Wide World Lecture Bureau, Inc.
  18 East 48 Street, New York, N. Y. 10017
    Tel. (212) PLaza 2-7747

  Some U. S. Government Agencies help with speakers; for example:

  U. S. Defense Department, Speakers Branch, Washington, D.C.
  Dr. David Smith, Director

  Office of Economic Opportunity, Washington, D.C.
  Mrs. Irene H. Mields, Director

  U. S. State Department, Division of Conferences and Speakers, Washington, D.C.
  Mr. John W. Piercy, Director

APPENDIX IV

RULES FOR DISPLAYING THE FLAG OF THE UNITED STATES OF AMERICA AT MEETINGS

(Adapted from the Official U. S. Code)
  When used on a speaker's platform, if displayed flat the flag should be placed above and behind the speaker.
  When displayed from a staff, it should occupy the position of honor and be placed at the speaker's right as he faces the audience. Any other flag on the platform should be placed at the speaker's left as he faces the audience.
  However, when the flag is displayed from a staff in a public auditorium elsewhere than on the platform, it should be placed in the position of honor at the right of the audience as they

face the platform. Any other flag so displayed should be on the left of the audience as they face the platform.

If other flags are displayed, none should be placed above or to the right of the U. S. flag.

If displayed with another flag against a wall from crossed staffs, the United States flag should be on the flag's own right, and the staff should be in front of the other flag's staff.

When flags of two or more nations are displayed, they are to be hung from separate staffs of the same height and the flags should be of approximately equal size.

The flag of the United States should be at the center and at the highest point of the group when a number of flags are displayed from staffs.

APPENDIX V

Sample of an informal invitation, sent to a mailing of 150.

Dear

Again this year the Friends of the Cleveland Public Library in cooperation with the public libraries of Greater Cleveland, the Commission on Higher Education, the Cleveland Chamber of Commerce, Higbee's, and the Women's National Book Association, will present a luncheon in observance of National Library Week.

Enclosed is a return card for your convenience.* As you will note, the luncheon will be held on Monday, April 18, at 12 noon, in Higbee's tenth floor Auditorium.

Tickets are $2.00 each, and tables are for eight. If your organization purchases one or more complete tables, a sign with your group's name will be placed on each.

Reservations may be made by calling CH 1-1020, Extension 161, or by mail addressed to the Director's Office. If you plan to attend, may we suggest that you make your reservations as soon as possible, since this luncheon has always been very popular.

----

* A program was also enclosed.

Please make checks payable to: Friends of the Cleveland Public Library.

We look forward to hearing from you.

Sincerely yours,

, *Chairman*

National Library Week

Luncheon Committee

Sample of card to be enclosed with the letter of invitation*

To: Reservations
     Cleveland Public Library
     325 Superior Avenue
     Cleveland, Ohio 44114

Please send me .... tickets for the National Library Week luncheon on April 18, 1966, at 12 Noon. A check for $........, payable to Friends of the Cleveland Public Library, Inc., is enclosed ($2.00 each, $16.00 for a table of eight).

    Name ....

    Address ....

    ....Zip No..........

    Telephone ....

Sample of Ticket

National

Library Week Luncheon

HIGBEE COMPANY AUDITORIUM

Monday, April 18, 1966   12 Noon

Table........
Tickets $2.00   No. (1 - 500)

Note: Ticket numbers were printed; table numbers were entered by hand after tickets were sorted into packs of eight.

---

* Note: the return card actually used was a printed one and repeated all luncheon details contained in the letter.

APPENDIX VI

Model Form of Introduction List Prepared by the
Program Chairman or Presiding Officer

ANNUAL LUNCHEON
OF THE BLANKVILLE UNIVERSITY CLUB

April 18, 19..

Presiding: Mr. Andrew Williams

INTRODUCTION OF SPEAKERS' TABLE

From Mr. Williams' right, audience's left:

Mr. William Broadby,* Superintendent of the County Public
Schools.

Mr. Edward Bailey, President, Board of Trustees, Blankville
Public Library.

Mr. Anthony Norman, News and Editorial Director, Television
Station ZAZ.

Mr. Charles Mann, Vice President, Blankville University Club.

Mr. Lawrence Wesley, Book Review Editor, Blankville News.

Miss Mary Dennis, Bookstore Manager, The Tilden Company.

Mr. Carl Raymond, Director, Blankville Public Library.

The next two, Miss Margaret Hall and Dr. Theodore Robertson,
are our speakers and will be introduced later.

Beginning with Mr. Williams' left, audience's right:

Mr. John Marks, President, The Blankville Civic League.

Mrs. David Jonas, Chairman, Blankville League of Women
Voters.

Dr. John Curtis, President, Rosedale College.

Mr. Horace Lee Jones, President, Blankville Chamber of Commerce.

Mr. Thomas Lockhart, Vice President, Blankville Bar Association.

Mr. Bartell Thompson, Editor, Blankville Evening Times.

Mrs. Charles Redman, Blankville's First Lady, representing her
husband, the Mayor, who was unable to attend.

---

* All names are fictitious.

The next two, Mrs. Seymour Cooke (our Program Chairman) and the Honorable Henry Jones, will be introduced later.

Applause after all have been introduced.

In this instance, the speakers were an educator, a judge, and a social worker, and outstanding representatives of these professions were invited to sit at the head table.

The fourth person to be introduced later was the program chairman, who in turn had the assignment of introducing the speakers.

Sample Introduction of Speaker

DR. THEODORE ROBERTSON

About a year ago I had the pleasure of hearing Dr. Theodore Robertson speak to a group interested primarily in college education. As I listened, I felt that what he was saying had implications for anyone involved or interested in the process of education at any level, and hoped that we might have him as our own luncheon speaker.

We succeeded in persuading Dr. Robertson to be with us today, and it is my privilege to introduce him to you.

Dr. Robertson became the fifth president of . . . . College in 1959, and his dynamic leadership of that well-known institution was quickly felt, both in the development of the college's physical plant and of the curriculum. One of his great innovations was the Spring Term Abroad for Juniors, which is . . . . . . 's most distinctive educational feature.

Before becoming President of . . . . College, Dr. Robertson was Dean at . . . . College.

He is a graduate of . . . . College, from which he holds a doctor of divinity degree. He has done extensive work at . . . . University.

His wide interests are reflected in his many activities: member of the American Academy of Political and Social Science, the American Philosophical Association, and others. He is a contributor to learned periodicals in the United States, Europe, and Asia, and is a member of the committee selecting scholars for fellowships in fields of international research and lecturing.

He is a member of the Board of Trustees of .... School, and Commodore of the River Yachting Club.

Dr. Robertson has a deep interest in international understanding, and has served as director of seminars in Sweden, France, and Israel. This interest has been largely responsible for the creation of his College's plan for sending its Juniors abroad.

This will be the basis, too, for the talk which we shall now hear—*Impressions of an Educator in Europe, 19..*—and I am most happy to present Dr. Theodore Robertson.

LIST OF GUESTS AT SPEAKERS' TABLE

Mr. Broadby
Mr. Bailey
Mr. Norman
Mr. Mann
Mr. Wesley
Miss Dennis
Mr. Raymond
Miss Hall
Mr. Robertson
Mr. Williams
Judge Jones
Mrs. Cooke
Mrs. Redman
Mr. Thompson
Mr. Lockhart
Mr. Jones
Dr. Curtis
Mrs. Jonas
Mr. Marks

A brief list of the guests in their order of seating is most helpful, and the following should be provided with copies: at the luncheon, the program chairman and the hostess or whoever has been delegated to set the place cards and assist with the seating; and prior to the event, the person who writes or prints (by hand) the place cards.

The above list has been arranged with the assumption that the lectern is a portable one set up after the meal. If it is a permanent installation, however, Mr. Williams will sit between it and Dr. Robertson, and on the other side, Mrs. Cooke and Judge Jones will exchange places.

In this model the clergy has not been represented. If an Invocation and a Benediction are to be included in the agenda, the clergymen will be placed: one on Mr. Williams' right between Miss Hall and Mr. Raymond, and the other on Mr. Williams' left between Mrs. Redman and Mr. Thompson.

APPENDIX VII

Sample Work Chart of Table Reservations

Row				Tables				
1.	BAR 1. ASSOC.	2. L.W.V.	COLLEGE 3. CLUB	S R. 4. CIT.	PRESS TABLE	CHAMBER OF 5. COMM.	6. WNBA.	7.
2.	15	CIVIC 14 LEAGUE 13		UNIV. 12 CLUB	TILDEN 11. Co.	PUB 10. LIB.	9	8.
3.	16	17	18	19	20	21	22	23
4.	31	30	29	28	27	26	25	24
5.	32	33	34	35	36	37	38	39
6.	47	46	45	44	43	42	41	40
7.	48	49	50	51	52	53	54	
8.	60	59	58	57	56	55		
9.	61	62	64	65	66			
10.	63	67						

Make an extra copy of the work chart, and a few days before the event send it to the person—the maitre d'hotel or his equivalent—who is in charge of setting up the tables. Check with that person a day before the meeting to make sure that everything is being done as scheduled.

SAMPLE WORK SHEET FOR
RECORDING PAYMENTS

(Yellow foolscap or any lined paper can be used)

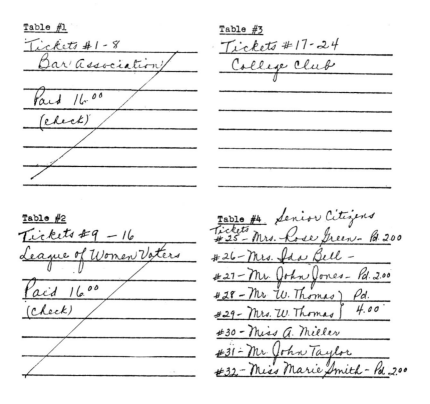

HOSTESS KEY TO TABLE
RESERVATION CHART

SPEAKERS' TABLE
SEATS 19

ROW	TABLES	TABLE ARRANGEMENT							
I	1 to 4 Press Table 5 to 7	1	2	3	4	Press Table	5	6	7
II	15 to 8	15	14	13	12	11	10	9	8
III	16 to 23	16	17	18	19	20	21	22	23
IV	31 to 24	31	30	29	28	27	26	25	24
V	32 to 39	32	33	34	35	36	37	38	39
VI	47 to 40	47	46	45	44	43	42	41	40
VII	48 to 54		48	49	50	51	52	53	54
VIII	60 to 55		60	59	58	57	56	55	
IX	61,62, 64-66		61	62	64	65	66		
X	63, 67 by doorway			63	67				

EVERY TICKET HAS THE TABLE NUMBER IN LOWER LEFT CORNER

EACH PERSON MUST SIT AT THE ASSIGNED TABLE

EACH TABLE RESERVED BY AN ORGANIZATION HAS A NAME SIGN

INDEX

105